MIDNIGHT MAYHEM

He heard screams before he heard the gunshots.

Raider raised up, listening. He had been sound asleep until the screams had echoed in the darkness. He wondered if he had been dreaming. Maybe it was part of some nightmare.

Someone moaned. The sound was more muffled than the screams. Raider thought for a moment that he was hearing the cries of a man and a woman making love.

Then he heard a dull thud.

Another high-pitched scream, quickly muffled.

Raider reached for his Colt . . .

RAIDER

TOMBSTONE
TERRITORY

J.D. HARDIN

B

BERKLEY BOOKS, NEW YORK

TOMBSTONE TERRITORY

A Berkley Book / published by arrangement with
the author

PRINTING HISTORY
Berkley edition / January 1990

ISBN: 0-425-11920-3

A BERKLEY BOOK ® TM 757,375
Berkley Books are published by The Berkley Publishing Group,
200 Madison Avenue, New York, New York 10016.
The name "BERKLEY" and the "B" logo
are trademarks belonging to the Berkley Publishing Corporation.

PRINTED IN THE UNITED STATES OF AMERICA

10 9 8 7 6 5 4 3 2 1

This book is dedicated to Kevin Sim.

CHAPTER ONE

A hot, dry wind pushed dust across the lone, empty street of Pearce, Territory of Arizona. Raider, the tall, black-eyed, rough-hewn Pinkerton agent from Arkansas, sat at the dirty window, peering out at the hole-in-the-wall town. His chest was bare, his feet were unshod. He wore only his chalky denim pants which were covered with a ghostly layer of prairie grit. Beside him, leaning against the wall, rested his Winchester rifle, oiled and loaded for action. His Colt six-shooter also hung on the wooden chair, a backup for the rifle.

"You look like a man who's ready for trouble," said the woman who lay in the bed behind him.

Raider just grunted. He was in no mood for chatter. Taking up with the woman had probably been a mistake anyway. She had come along at a time when he had temporarily sworn off the weaker sex. His luck with females had not been running very well, so leave it to fate to cast her straight into his arms, the only whore in Pearce.

"You some kind of law?" she asked, shifting the sheet over her large breasts. "I mean, all you do is watch the street."

"Look, Betty," the big man said without looking back, "why don't—"

"My name's Beth!" she insisted. "Call me Beth."

He glanced over his shoulder. Her red lips were drawn tightly into a pout. Short, thin hair that was as sandy as the street, big thighs and hips and chest, the way Raider liked them. Not as pretty as some, but better than most.

Raider turned back toward the street. "Never mind, honey. Think you could rustle me up some grub?"

Beth sighed. "Eat, sleep, and top me. That's all you done since you got here. And watch that damned street. Two days you been watchin' that street."

"I paid you, ain't I?"

"Well, yes. But a girl still wants a man to pay attention to her. I mean, I'm kinda gettin' to like you."

The big Pinkerton exhaled impatiently. "Yeah, we're a couple o' real lovebirds. Think you could lay two eggs over easy an' some bacon?"

She shifted on the bed, coming out from under the covers. He heard her steps on the floor. Warm hands on his shoulders. Her breasts draped over him as she leaned down.

"Come on back to bed," she whispered in his ear. "You can do it to me again. That whanger of yours is about the biggest I ever seen."

He shrugged her away. "Betty—"

"Beth!"

"All right, Beth. Just listen t' me a minute. I got work t' do an' mostly it means watchin' this street."

She stepped back a few feet, covering her nipples with her hands. "I knew it! You're a lawman! Or a bounty hunter!"

Raider shook his head. "No, I'm a Pinkerton agent. And I'm lookin' for a boy name o' Johnny Blackfist."

"Johnny!"

He turned to regard her. "You know him?"

She nodded. "That bastard is the low-downedest son of a bitch that ever shit in a hole in the ground."

Raider turned back to the window, gazing out at the street again.

"I'm after Blackfist," he said. "He's got kin in these parts and I'm hopin' he'll show."

"That half-breed coyote," Beth went on. "Why, I had him

once and he didn't even pay me. Just rode out laughin'."

Raider smiled. "He any good?"

"Not as good as you, lover."

She put her hands on his shoulders again.

Raider shrugged her off. "Honey, not now."

"Later?" she asked hopefully.

"Mebbe. If you get me some grub."

She hurried to put on some clothes. "I'll do anythin' to help you catch that half-breed bastard."

So Blackfist was a breed, Raider thought. The telegram from the home office hadn't mentioned that. Raider had suspected when he heard the name, but there had been no way to be sure.

He looked back at the woman, who was busy cramming her bosom into a dress that seemed to be too tight for her. "Is he Apache?"

She smiled and nodded. "His mother was Indian. But she's dead. Some say Johnny killed her hisself, but I don't believe it. Even a snake like him wouldn't kill his own mother."

Raider peered out at the street again. "His pa still alive?"

"No, but he has some cousins in these parts. Leastways that's what I heard. Don't know if it's true or not."

Raider had heard the same thing. Two cousins, only they didn't live in town. Nobody knew exactly where they lived. The tribe—what was left of it—wouldn't take them in and no white men wanted to have anything to do with them. They were homeless, lawless, renegade half-breeds, just like Johnny.

"Why they call him Blackfist?" Raider asked.

Beth shrugged, but then her face wrinkled. "Maybe it's 'cause he always wears a pair of black leather gloves."

"Makes sense."

"I'm goin' for breakfast," Beth offered. "And when I get back, you better be ready for me."

"I sure will be, honey. I sure will be."

The door slammed as she went out. Not a bad room, Raider thought. Beth lived atop a clean, well-tended general store. The town also sported a livery and a saloon, neither of which were as neat as the store. But the livery had served to stable his gray gelding and the saloon had rendered up a bottle of whiskey that didn't burn too badly as it went down. Raider

had shared a couple of drinks with the woman, but he was
going easy on the drinking. Best to stay sober, at least until he
caught Johnny Blackfist.

He sighed, leaning back in the chair. The search for the
half-breed hadn't gone too well. Raider had been in Tucson
when the wire cam from Wagner at the home office. There
were special instructions from the territorial governor and
from the marshal for the Arizona territory. Blackfist was to be
apprehended immediately, dead or alive. The renegade had
been terrorizing settlers and prospectors all over the territory.
And Blackfist didn't seem to fear anyone or anything. He
hadn't run over the border to Mexico, nor had he gone into
one of the neighboring territories. He had been striking in a
circle all around Pearce, but Raider had not been able to catch
him.

Five weeks, he thought, and still no results. What would
William Wagner and Allan Pinkerton say if Raider let Blackfist escape? So far in his wild tenure as an agent, Raider had
never let a man get away. But there was always that first time.
It happened to every agent sooner or later. A man naturally
slowed down as he got older, lost a step here and there. Of
course, he could make the adjustment, relying on his wits
instead of quickness. Still, given a choice between the two
alternatives, Raider would always choose quickness in the
face of trouble.

"Damn," he said.

Dust whirled around in the street, as if the devil himself
was stirring it. It didn't look good. Blackfist could be anywhere by now. Coming to Pearce had been a last-ditch idea.
Raider wasn't even sure he would recognize the outlaw if he
saw him. Except for the black leather gloves that the woman
had mentioned. That might help eventually. But Raider had to
find him first.

The door swung open behind him. Raider reached for the
rifle, levering a round into the chamber. Beth gasped wide-
eyed at the bore of the Winchester.

"Sorry," the big man said, leaning the rifle against the wall
again.

"Thought you were gonna shoot me," she said, her breasts
heaving.

Raider shrugged. "Didn't mean t' scare you."

"That's all right," she replied. "It was kinda excitin'."

She carried the tray to him. Raider could smell the bacon. When she put the food in front of him, he tried to eat slowly but his appetite got the best of him. He was surprised that she had come up with biscuits and gravy.

Beth watched as he gulped down the food. "You're as hungry over the plate as you are in bed."

He handed the empty plate back to her. "Thanks."

"Was it good?"

Raider nodded. "Where the hell did you find fresh bacon like that in this hellhole town?"

"The storekeeper," she replied. "He gets it from Tombstone."

Raider grimaced. "Tombstone. Don't like that place much. Dangerous silver country."

"So I been told," Beth replied. "Can't be worse'n here, though."

Raider belched and wiped his mouth with the back of his hand. "Does the storekeeper take pretty good care o' you?"

She sighed, putting the plate on top of the dresser. "We have a deal," she replied. "He lets me stay here and I give him a share of what I make. When business is bad, he takes his rent in trade. Course, that don't bother me. He finishes pretty quick and then he goes back downstairs."

"I wonder if he knows Blackfist?"

"As much as most," Beth replied. "But he don't trash too much with Johnny. Nobody does. I reckon when he comes to town, ever'body just hopes he don't rob or kill somebody. We sure could use a sheriff 'round here."

Raider glanced back at her to ask another question, but Beth was stepping out of her dress, prompting him to forget his inquiry. She grinned when his eyes fell on her. Raider felt the stiffening in his jeans. Sometimes his manly urges got in the way of business. He was always having to make the choice between women and work.

"Like what you see?" she asked.

"Yeah, I reckon."

She slid into bed. "Come on. It won't take all day. You can watch that window for the rest of the day."

The wind picked up suddenly, blowing thicker dust devils

in the street. Raider saw movement in the distance. He reached slowly for his rifle.

Beth saw him grab the gun. "What is it?"

"Shh. Wait a minute before you start jabberin'."

She pulled the sheet indignantly over her breasts. "You can't talk to me like that—"

The sound of the Winchester's hammer rippled through the room, silencing the offended lady.

A slight smirk spread over the big man's rugged face, barely disturbing the thick, black moustache above his upper lip. Maybe this was it. Maybe it was Johnny Blackfist riding slowly into Pearce.

Two riders emerged from the dust clouds. Slow and steady, they moved toward town. They wore serapes and wide-brimmed Stetsons.

Raider called back to the girl. "When Blackfist was with you, did he dress like a Mexican?"

"I don't know."

"Bullshit," the big man replied, wheeling to scowl at her. "Women always pay attention t' what people wear. Was Blackfist dressed like a Mexican pistolero?"

She thought about it but then shook her head. "No, more like a Mexican rancher. You know, high waistcoat and pointed boots. Tight pants too."

"I bet you liked that."

"Kiss my ass!" she cried.

He chortled. "I may do that if this thing works out."

Turning back to the window, he saw the riders as they came up the street. Their faces were dark and dirty, but their features were not cut like those of an Apache. Raider called the woman to the window. He asked her to look down, to see if she recognized them.

Her stringy, straw-colored hair shook as she nodded. "That's Julio Valero Vasquez," she said. "The other one is his brother."

"Who are they?"

Beth shrugged. "Ah, you know, farmers, I guess. They got a hut between here and Tombstone. They work sometimes, sometimes they run cattle over the border. Good boys, really."

Raider studied the two brothers, trying to discern the presence of firearms beneath their serapes. "Do they know Black-fist?"

"Yeah, but they wouldn't ride with him."

The big man glanced up at her. "Why?"

"Well, there used to be three Vasquez brothers. If you get what I mean."

Raider smiled, turning his attention back to the street. If Blackfist had indeed killed one of the Vasquez boys, his surviving brothers might be useful. He'd have to give it some thought.

Beth leaned over, kissing him on the forehead. "Come on back to bed for a little while."

He turned toward her and his face brushed against the erect nipples of her breasts.

Raider tried to swallow. "I gotta watch."

She smiled. "No you don't. This little ol' pissant town is so small that a boll weevil couldn't crawl through it without makin' a ruckus."

She had a point there, he thought.

"Why, a walking horse makes a noise," she offered. "Close your eyes and listen. You can hear the hooves of the Vasquez boys' horses."

He closed his eyes just to make sure she was right.

"Johnny Blackfist ain't gonna sneak in and out of Pearce without you knowin' about it," Beth went on. "Why, he's— Hey, what are you doin'?"

Raider had risen to his feet, taking her forearm. "You make a lotta sense, girl. An' you smell good too. What happened? Did the storekeeper give you a free bottle o' lilac water?"

Before she could answer, he led her to the bed.

Beth fell gleefully onto the feather mattress, lying back with her head on the pillow as Raider unbuckled his belt. Her breasts flowed to both sides of her chest, her thighs parted to reveal the pink cleft at the center of her crotch. Raider's pants hit the floor. He slid down next to her.

Beth's hand closed around the thickness of his cock. "I won't even charge you this time."

He lowered his mouth to her nipples.

"Feel between my legs," she said. "I'm wet an' ready."

Raider touched her, feeling her body tense when his finger brushed the soft pebble at the entrance to her vagina. He wasn't sure what it was called, he just knew that women went wild if you touched them there. He would never have known about it if a whore hadn't shown him. Whores were the only kind of women who talked about such things.

Her teeth nibbled at his ear. "I ain't had it like this since I was over in Tombstone."

Raider hesitated. "Damn."

Beth looked into his eyes. "What?"

"Tombstone," he said. "Never liked the sound of that town. Never been there but once."

She cradled his face into her chest. "Don't worry about it. Just put that thing of yours where it belongs."

"Honey, that's just what I'm gonna do."

He climbed onto her, parting her legs further, guiding the head of his prick to the entrance of her cunt. Beth reached down to give him a hand. He felt the opening, the soft petals of her flower.

Beth gazed up at him heavy-lidded eyes. "All the way, cowboy. All the fuckin' way."

He obliged her, impaling her with a slow thrust.

She gasped, throwing back her head, lifting her legs to the ceiling.

As Raider began to move, the woman writhed under him, following his every motion with a shifting rythmn of her own. They panted as if they had been running from some dark, sinister foe. The woman cried out, announcing her pleasure to anyone within earshot.

Raider grabbed the sides of the mattress, holding on as she bucked him like a wild pony. His own sap began to rise, emptying into her as he gave one loud groan. She rasped, like someone had drawn a knife across her skin. Her face was frozen, locked in the mask of pleasant agony.

Her arms closed around him when he collapsed on top of her.

"Don't pull it out yet," she begged. "Leave it in until it's soft."

Raider probably would have obeyed her, but in the next instant, the sound of horse's hooves resounded from the street below.

As quickly as he could move, Raider was up and at the window.

"Hey!" the woman cried.

Raider exhaled. "It's nobody," he said. "Just a farmer on a draft horse. Wearin' a straw hat."

"That'd be Ben Wilson," she said nonchalantly.

"You know ever' man in the ter'tory?"

Beth shrugged. "Hey, it's my business, ain't it?"

He winked at her. "And you do a good job, honey."

She smiled at him. "Thanks for appreciatin' a good thing. I mean, a man could do worse than to have a wife like me, you know."

Raider winced at the word *wife*, although when he thought about it, it shouldn't have surprised him. They all came to it sooner or later. It was in their natures.

"Come on back to bed," she entreated.

Raider shook his head and picked up his pants. "Naw. It's back t' street watchin' for me."

"Later?"

He nodded. "Yeah. Why not?"

"I won't even take any other customers," she offered.

Raider grimaced. "Hey, honey, don't let me interfere with bus'ness. You gotta make a livin' like the rest of us."

She frowned, which probably meant the end of the wife talk.

Raider pulled on his pants, buttoning his fly.

Beth was poised to say something else, but the rattling of tack came up over the whirring of the wind.

Raider eased back to the window, expecting to see the farmer again. The big man winced when he gazed down on the rider. It was a tall man, riding a brown-and-white pinto. He had features like an Apache and copper-colored skin. Raider reached for the Winchester when he saw the black-gloved hands that held the reins of the pinto.

"Who is it?" the woman asked.

"Johnny Blackfist," Raider replied. "An' he's ridin' straight down Main Street toward the saloon."

CHAPTER TWO

In the stately offices of the Pinkerton National Detective Agency, Allan Pinkerton paced back and forth on a dais that had been raised so he could, as William Wagner had put it, "address the troops." Wagner had arranged for the largest collection of Pinkerton agents ever to gather in the home office. More than fifty in all, with the numbers growing even as Pinkerton stepped up to the podium in front of him.

"Gentlemen," he said in a booming voice. "I—"

Pinkerton stopped, gazing down at a short, pudgy man who slid into the seat next to William Wagner. The little man stared sheepishly at the floor, hoping the sturdy Scotsman would not dress him down in front of the others. His name was Henry Stokes and he had come a long way for the meeting.

"How nice of you to join us," Wagner said from the corner of his mouth.

Stokes tried not to smile. "Where's Raider?" he asked. "I don't see him."

Pinkerton cleared his throat and looked out over the gathering. "Gentlemen, I am delighted to welcome you to Chicago. I've never seen this many of our men in one room."

The agents erupted in applause and whooping calls.

Pinkerton allowed them their moment of self-aggrandizement and then went on with his speech. "But my delight in welcoming you here is the only thing I'm happy about today. For we've a serious task ahead of us—"

Henry Stokes leaned back, twirling his black derby in his hand. He had heard the speech from the old man before. Stokes had really caught hell after a certain incident in east Texas, the first and only time he had worked with Raider. It was always the same snake oil sale—agents had to be smarter, less violent; they had to be professionals. Stokes wondered if the old man really believed what he was saying. Everybody knew that it was rough in the field. Sometimes violence was the only way to settle things.

"—representing his agency, an agency that bears my name—"

Stokes closed his eyes.

Wagner nudged him with an elbow. "You're snoring!"

Stokes righted himself and sat up straight.

The old man was staring down at him. "—and it is *your* duty, *Mister* Stokes—"

The others smiled and snickered at Henry's misfortune. Not that they all hadn't been in the fire just like him. Who hadn't faced the wrath of the bearded Scotsman? It was part of the job.

Pinkerton lifted his disapproving gaze from Henry Stokes and went on with his speech. They listened with respect and interest, wondering how seriously to take Pinkerton. Sure, he had to say it, but in the field you often made quick judgments, especially when you were staring down the barrel of a six-gun.

"And in conclusion, let me say it is my wish that you all cooperate to the letter of the law with all local constabularies—"

A groan from the crowd.

"I mean it!" Pinkerton urged. "Every one of you has a duty to uphold the reputation of this agency. I will not have you going against the law, whether it be a local sheriff or the special agents of the United States Government. You will cooperate!"

They applauded him to make sure it was the end.

Pinkerton then walked among them, shaking hands and congratulating men who had earned his appreciation. Though he could be stern, the bearded giant of a man was fair and understanding. None of his men would have openly admitted affection for the boss, but they all loved him in a way a foot soldier loves a great general.

He approached Henry Stokes, who smiled tentatively.

"Hello, Mr. Pinkerton."

The Scotsman glared at Stokes, but then said, "Good job in Nebraska, Stokes. Clever work."

Stokes smiled broadly. "Thank you, sir. Thank you!"

Pinkerton went past him, talking to another smiling agent.

Wagner moved next to Stokes. "You did a fine job out there, Henry. Those farmers are grateful to you."

Stokes shrugged. "Ah, I just figured it out. The marshals took care of the rest. Caught those jayhawkers and let them have it. I just figured out where they were hiding."

"No Indians?" Wagner asked.

Stokes shook his head. "Nope. The gang wanted everybody to believe it was like that, but I knew better. Too many different kinds of Indian stuff had been planted. It seemed obvious after I thought about it."

"Are you ready for another case?" Wagner asked.

When Stokes nodded, Wagner ushered the pudgy little man into Allan Pinkerton's private office.

"There's trouble in New Orleans," Wagner said. "This came in today. Here; read it."

Stokes took his time, nodding. "Murders, huh? Too many. The local boys can't solve it."

Wagner bristled. "Now look here, you heard what Pinkerton said about cooperating with local law enforcement officials."

Stokes whistled through his teeth. "Yeah, I know all about it. We clean out their stables and then they pose for a picture with the shit-shovel."

"Watch your language!"

"Sorry, Wagner. I heard the old man."

"Mister Pinkerton!"

"Sure, sure."

Wagner pointed a finger at him. "You could be fired for such impertinence."

"I said I was sorry."

Wagner sighed, shaking his head defeatedly. "You and Raider! Why don't I just ashcan both of you! You're both disrespectful, unkempt—"

"We get the job done," Stokes said defensively. "And speakin' of the big galoot, where the devil is he?"

"Arizona," Wagner replied. "Chasing a man named Johnny Blackfist. I haven't heard from him in a month."

Stokes rubbed his fat chin. "A month, huh? Maybe I better take a run out there and see if he's—"

"New Orleans," Wagner insisted. "I want you to be on the first train that heads south. Do you understand?"

Stokes sighed. "Yeah."

There was an awkward moment of silence.

"Is there something on your mind, Henry?"

Stokes shifted nervously on his feet. "I was thinkin'. After that business in east Texas, I thought me and Raider made a pretty good team."

"Don't remind me of that," Wagner said with a groan. "It was all I could do to talk the railroad company out of making the agency pay for the train that you and Raider crashed."

"Raider did it!"

Wagner waved him out of the office. "New Orleans, Henry."

"So I ain't gonna work with Raider?"

Wagner shook his head. "He'd never allow it. You know that."

"But—"

"New Orleans!"

Stokes hurried out of the office.

Wagner sat down for a moment, taking a breather. Lately things had been hectic at the agency; a sign of good business. And then Pinkerton had to go and call the meeting, taking most of their agents out of the field. Of course, Raider was still working.

Wagner was glad that the rough-hewn hillbilly had not shown for the big powwow. The meeting had gone a lot smoother without him. Raider could be a lot of trouble— especially for men he was chasing: men like Johnny Blackfist.

CHAPTER THREE

When Raider saw Johnny Blackfist, his first inclination was to put the barrel through the window and start firing. But he knew that probably wouldn't be the best thing to do. Best to watch, wait, study on it. There were other citizens in Pearce who had to be considered. It was always better to take an outlaw without shooting if you could pull it off.

Easing the window open, he slid out onto the roof that slanted down over the porch of the general store. Pausing, he peered toward the pinto as it walked down the dusty street. Blackfist was going to wet his whistle at the saloon. That might be a good place to take him. Just wander in pretending to be a thirsty cowboy, then put the Colt to his temple and tell him to hold real still.

Blackfist halted the pinto at the hitching rail in front of the saloon.

Raider felt a hand on the back of his neck. He turned with the rifle, sticking the barrel in Beth's pretty face.

"Don't shoot me," she whimpered.

Sweat poured off the big man's forehead. "Damn it, woman, git back in there b'fore I—"

Beth moved back toward the bed.

Raider looked at Blackfist again. The outlaw was tying the pinto's reins around the hitching rail. Raider crouched low and then went belly-down on the roof. He expected Blackfist to head straight through the swinging doors of the saloon, but instead the half-breed Apache wheeled and walked toward the general store, where Raider waited with the girl.

"Damn," he whispered.

Blackfist's spurs clinked as he stepped onto the porch. Raider eased back into the room, trying to move without any noise so the outlaw wouldn't hear him on the roof overhead. Beth grabbed him as he started for the door.

"What are you doing?"

Raider gently pushed her aside. "I'm gonna take Blackfist. He just walked into the store."

"Be careful."

Raider lifted a finger to his lips. "Git my shirt," he whispered, "an' my boots."

He was going to look like any other cowboy leaving the company of the local girl for hire. Sling his holster over his shoulder so he wouldn't be pegged as a gunfighter. Carry the rifle in one hand. Smile broadly at Blackfist, maybe even exchange some pleasantries, enough to get within striking distance.

Beth worked the buttons of his shirt. "Don't shoot the storekeeper," she entreated. "It's took me a long time to get it this good, so don't mess it up for me."

Raider shifted the holster on his shoulder, making sure he could execute a cross-draw if he had to.

Beth kissed him on the cheek. "Be careful."

He took a deep breath. Just go slow, put the barrel of the Colt on his neck. Fire if he had to. Take him alive if possible.

Of course, sometimes things didn't work out as well as they're planned.

Raider opened the door of the room. "Well, punkin," he said in a loud voice, "that was sure all right by me."

Beth acted the way he had coached her. "Oh, you come back any time now, sugar. Don't be a stranger."

Raider winked at her and started noisily down the stairs. He wanted Blackfist to know he was coming. No surprise, at least not until he was close enough to the Apache.

Blackfist looked up when Raider came into the store.

The big man winked at him. "Been havin' me some o' the good stuff, stranger. Know what I mean?"

Blackfist snapped his head back to look at the storekeeper. "The girl? Is she free?"

The storekeeper nodded.

Raider laughed, pausing at the end of the counter. "She ain't free, pardner, but she's available."

Blackfist shot him a dirty look.

Raider just ignored it as he studied the thin gunslinger. Johnny was dressed just as Beth had described him. He resembled a Spanish rancher. A shiny new Remington .44 hung low on his leg. Left-handed. Raider wondered if Blackfist could handle a gun with those gloves on.

Johnny glanced back at the storekeeper. "I want the girl." He threw five silver dollars on the counter. "For her and the bullets."

Raider whistled. "Boy, they charged me a lot lower price than that. But, I guess you know what you're doin'."

Blackfist picked up one of the dollars. "Four."

The storekeeper was in no mood to argue.

Raider knew the breed was going to have to move past him to get to the woman. He turned toward the counter, putting his back to the outlaw. Make it seem like he wasn't interested in Blackfist, then when the Indian passed, grab him and put the Colt to his head.

"You want the cartridges now?" the storekeeper asked.

Blackfist nodded.

Raider held his breath, waiting. It seemed to take the storekeeper a long time to get back with the bullets. Then Blackfist insisted on opening the box to make sure all the brass shells were there.

Blackfist drew his weapon quickly, ending any questions about his prowess with the gloves on. He opened the pistol and loaded two shells into empty chambers. Low on ammo, Raider thought.

The storekeeper was nervous, even after Blackfist holstered the Remington.

Raider had to be quick, get the gun, pin his hands.

The half-breed's boots clomped on the wooden floor.

Time the turn just right, the big man thought.

Blackfist passed him.

Raider wheeled, cross-drawing the Colt. Using his superior weight, he shoved Blackfist into the wall, causing the half-breed to grunt as the air left his lungs. Raider pressed the bore of the six-gun against the outlaw's temple.

"Don't flinch, Johnny, or the store man will be cleanin' your brains off the walls."

Blackfist whimpered like a dog. "Don't kill me. Please."

"You're gonna see the end of a rope," Raider said. "But if you act like a gentleman, I won't be the one t' kill you. I got nothin' agin you personal-like, Johnny, I'm just an honest Pinkerton doin' a day's work."

He reached down to draw the Remington from Blackfist's holster.

Johnny seemed to recover a little. "You Pinkerton bastard."

Raider thumbed the hammer of his Colt. "Put your hands back here. Go on. I'll pull this trigger if you don't."

Blackfist obeyed the big man. Raider had to grin. It was going fine. Nothing to worry about.

Until the shooting started.

"You feelthy peeg! You keeled our brother, you half-breed bastard!"

Twin Navy Colts rang out from the entrance of the general store. Slugs chopped holes in the wall next to Johnny Black-fist's head. The Vasquez brothers had come to exact their revenge, only they weren't very good shots.

Raider started to turn to face them. Blackfist felt the weight lifting off him. Immediately the outlaw began to squirm, trying to wriggle free.

"Keel heem!"

"Damn it!" the big man cried, "I ain't—"

· But the Vasquez brothers had no intention of listening. They emptied their weapons, missing Raider and the outlaw despite their efforts to take careful aim. Still, in the barrage of flying lead, Raider was not inclined to stay on his feet. He dived for the floor, trying to drag Blackfist with him.

But the outlaw managed to break away from Raider's hold on him. He dug across the floor, diving headlong through the side window. Raider started to rise to chase him, but the Vasquez brothers had finished reloading.

More shots flew over the big man's head.

"Damn it, you gopher-heads! Didn't you see Blackfist go out the window?"

The pistols stopped.

Raider could hear hoofbeats driving away. Blackfist had reached his horse in time to get a head start. Raider's own mount was still in the livery, so he'd have to waste more time getting ready to ride.

The Vasquez brothers fired shots after the fleeing outlaw. They turned to fire again at Raider as he was about to get up. His belly hit the floor again.

"Damn it, you two! I'm a Pinkerton agent. I come here t' take Blackfist in for hangin'!"

The brothers talked it over in Spanish.

"We do not believe you, señor! We theenk you are with Blackfist."

Raider felt the Colt, which was still in hand. "All right, boys. I don't wanna kill you, but if you insist—"

He rolled to his left and came up firing.

One of the Vasquez brothers cried out in pain.

"No mas!" the other one cried, dropping his weapon.

The wounded brother held up his hands. "You have shot me, señor!"

Raider scrambled to his feet. "Well, what the hell'd you expect me to do? I gave you a chance t' surrender."

"Please, señor, do not keel us."

He strode toward the Mexicans, looking for damage. His shot had clipped the man's hand. There was plenty of blood, but the man would live.

"Like I told you, I'm a Pinkerton agent. I ain't gonna shoot nobody. Hell, I oughta let both o' you have it. Thanks t' you, Blackfist got away without a hitch."

The unwounded man took off his hat. "He keeled our brother, señor. When he rode into town, we wanted to sneak up on heem."

Raider took a deep breath. "Hell, I reckon I cain't blame you. Even if you did mess it up for me, you was just tryin' t' get the man who killed your kin. I still wish you hadn't shot at us."

"Thank you, señor."

"Don't thank me just yet," the big man said. "I may need your help."

"Anything, señor, if it weell breeng that peeg to the gallows."

Raider tipped back his Stetson, peering to the southwest, the same direction in which Blackfist had fled. "You boys know these parts pretty good. Where's that half-breed headin'?"

"Tombstone," one of the Mexicans replied.

Raider winced. He didn't even like the sound of the name. How could a man like the name of a town that was going to be sitting on his grave some day?

"Keel him for us, señor."

The Vasquez brothers turned to head for the saloon, to find a bandage and a bottle of whiskey.

Raider went back into the store to retrieve the things he had dropped during the gunfire.

The storekeeper stuck his head up from behind the counter. "Is the shootin' over?"

"Yeah."

Beth tiptoed down the stairs, peeking into the room. "Raider?"

"I'm still alive, honey."

She ran to him, wrapping her arms around his shoulders. "I heard all the shootin'," she said. "I thought you was dead."

"The Vasquez brothers ain't very handy with guns," he replied, "Else I'd be dead on the floor."

"They were tryin' to plug Blackfist for killin' their brother," the storekeeper chimed in. "Lordy, we got to get a sheriff for this danged town. Heck, even Tombstone has a new marshal. Man by the name of Earp."

Raider didn't hear the name of the new marshal. He knew he had to get into the saddle. Blackfist wasn't that far ahead of him. And the trail would be easy to follow.

Beth held tight, not wanting to let him go. "You could have been killed, Raider. Don't follow him. Come upstairs with me."

He pushed her away. "So long, honey. I'll see you next time 'round. No hard feelin's."

"Earp!" the storekeeper cried as Raider made his exit. "They say he's a real tough one."

The warm wind blew up again as Raider strode across the street to the livery. The smith stood over the anvil, banging a heavy hammer on a piece of iron that glowed red. He frowned when he saw the tall Pinkerton standing in his stable.

Raider felt a familiar churning in his stomach—the feeling that always came before something went wrong.

"I was hopin' you was gonna come tomorrow," the smith said.

Raider glanced toward the stall where his gray munched oats from a feed bag. "What's the trouble?"

"Split shoe on the gray," the smith said. "Take me till this evenin' to get it ready. May have to treat that hoof."

"Damn. I cain't wait. What else you got back there?"

The smithy frowned. "Come again?"

"Another mount, honcho. How much?"

"Uh—I ain't sure. I got a sorrel mare."

Raider nodded. "Okay, what's the damages?"

"I don't understand."

The big man from Arkansas was losing patience. "You take the gray. Give me the sorrel. What's the difference in price? And what do I owe you in stable charges?"

The livery man licked his dry, cracked lips. "Twenty dollars." He said it like he thought Raider was going to give him a hard time.

Instead, a twenty dollar gold piece glittered as it flew through the air. The man caught the double eagle and bit into the coin to determine its authenticity. He seemed satisfied with the deal, as if he had taken advantage of Raider's necessity.

"I shined your saddle too," he said as Raider threw it over the back of the sorrel. "She's a mite skittish, but she can run."

"I hope so, pardner. I sure as hell hope so."

He felt better when he was in the saddle, riding south. He wondered how far it was to Tombstone.

The hair raised on the back of his neck. He hated the sound of the word. Tombstone. A place where trouble always stopped for a drink and a woman.

CHAPTER FOUR

The sorrel mare held up well in the heat. She moved steadily against the dry, gritty wind that sanded Raider's rugged face. He pulled a bandanna over his mouth and nose, wishing the damned wind would stop. He had no idea how far he was from Tombstone.

An eddy of dust swirled around him, causing the mare to snort and whinny. He patted the mare's neck and gave her a few words of encouragement.

They headed steadily southwest, riding against the hot wind.

Nothing seemed to be going right. Raider couldn't even find a trail to follow. As soon as Johnny Blackfist's mount made a track, the breeze blew it away. Raider felt a little better when he saw a pile of fresh horse manure, although there was no way to determine whether or not it belonged to Blackfist's pinto. At least it was something.

Keep steady. Don't get too riled. Raider had been on trails like this a hundred times or more. See it through. He'd find Blackfist sooner or later. The damned territory wasn't that big.

The plain appeared to be boiling under the hot wind. He

21

might miss Tombstone in the dust. What if Blackfist didn't go to Tombstone? It wouldn't hurt at all to get quickly in and out of the dismal town.

But something told Raider that Johnny Blackfist would be there, mainly because it was just like an outlaw to run to a place that the big man loathed.

Tombstone.

He hated the name and the damned town.

The wind eased later in the day. There were still gusts of pitting velocity, but for the most part the breeze just stirred sheets of low-blowing sand that chipped at the mare's legs. Raider got down to wrap her forelegs, trying to keep her as comfortable as possible. She didn't look like much, but she was strong.

Back in the saddle, he began to consider what he was going to do if he didn't reach Tombstone before nightfall. If he camped on the plain, he might wake up buried in sand or worse yet, he might not wake up at all. Of course, with the mare under him, he could ride through the night, which meant possibly missing the town altogether in the dark. If the wind picked up again, the few dim lights of Tombstone might not be visible at night. How much sunlight left? Three hours?

"Tombstone," he muttered.

Why did he hate the town so much? He hadn't been in any trouble there. So why did it give him a numb sensation down his spine when he heard the damned name come out of his mouth?

Just a feel for the place, he decided. Sometimes a town just gave you a funny itching in your craw. Yuma and Helena always gave him the same uneasy quiver in his gut. But Tombstone had to be the worst.

He had almost decided to stop for a while when he saw the hand-painted signpost. It read, "Tombstone, Two Miles or Less." Right beside the sign rested another pile of manure. From Blackfist's pinto?

Raider spurred the mare, figuring he would know in two miles or less.

•   •   •

The wind picked up again, but Raider pushed on until he saw a slight rise emerge from the boiling cloud of dust. He slowed, riding at the base of the ridge, knowing he was close to Tombstone but still unable to see it through the grit. The mare snorted and tossed her head.

Raider patted her neck, looking to the right and left. "What you smell, girl? Water or oats?"

It was water. A wooden trough appeared out of nowhere. It was full and a little dirty, but the mare didn't care. She plunged her muzzle into the water for a long drink.

Raider dismounted, pulling her face out of the trough so she wouldn't make herself sick. He turned to his left, glancing up the incline. He saw something vague and ghostly at the top of the rise.

"Best to have a look," he said to the mare.

She didn't want to leave the trough but Raider pulled her to the crest of the sandy knoll. He saw the arch that had been raised as an entrance to the graveyard. "Boot Hill" had been painted on a piece of board and nailed to the split rails that had been used to make the arch. Raider studied the wooden crosses and tombstones that marked the graves of the unfortunate dead men. A few of the mounds looked fresh, as if the corpses had been recently laid to rest.

Raider turned and gazed to the southwest again. From the top of Boot Hill, he could see the rooftops of Tombstone as they spread out in the dust. The town was bigger than Pearce, a lot bigger. Too many places for a man like Johnny Blackfist to hide.

What was it the storekeeper had said before he left Pearce? Something about a new marshal in Tombstone. Raider couldn't remember the name. He figured a lawman wouldn't make much difference in a place like Tombstone. The silver boom had done it, had made the town spring up in the middle of the Arizona plain. Silver. Demon silver. The dull grey metal that shined into something worth a lot of money. Raider hated silver. He had never trusted it or what it did to men.

No, a marshal wouldn't make much difference in a silver town. Unless he had a fast gun hand and didn't mind killing on a daily basis. Best to go in, find Blackfist and get the hell out.

He led the mare down from Boot Hill, mounted, and then rode toward the vague shapes and angles that stood defiantly against the Arizona wind.

The place didn't seem as bad when Raider finally guided the mare toward a livery stable on the edge of town. A bright fire illuminated the stable and a smiling blacksmith made him welcome. Raider had to wonder what he had been worrying about. Maybe Tombstone wasn't that bad after all.

"How's the mare fixed for shoes?" the smith asked.

Raider shrugged. "She's fine. Mebbe you could tell me where I might find a place t' sleep."

"There's the hotel," the smith replied. "Or at least we call it a hotel. I got a loft upstairs that's better'n the worst room they got over there. Charge you two bits a day to sleep here."

"I might take you up on that. But for now, get the mare taken care of. I'd also be much obliged if you'd find me a bottle o' gun oil."

The smith's eyes narrowed. "Look here; I don't want no trouble."

Raider reached into his pocket, pulling out a silver dollar. He flipped it to the livery man and told him there would be no trouble. Just find him a bottle of gun oil, if that was all right.

"Sure, partner. Sure."

Raider then unwrapped his weapons which had been protected by a thick cloth to keep the grit out of them. Sand could do a year's damage to a Colt and a Winchester. Both guns had come out of the dust without any noticeable wear.

The smith came toward him with a bottle of oil. "Nice rifle," he told Raider. "And that Colt is just as good. What kind of wood is that on the handle?"

"Redwood," the big man replied. "Carved it myself."

The smith went back to his forge, stoking the fire. "Well, I reckon you ain't a gunslinger," he offered.

Raider eyed him sideways. "Why you say that?"

The smith shrugged. "No notches on your gun. Reckon you ain't killed too many men."

Raider went back to oiling his firearms. No need to say he had killed more than his share. He knew the smith was trying to draw him out and there was no reason to give him any gossip to spread around town.

"You a prospector?" the smith asked.

"I'm lookin' for someone," Raider replied. "You seen a boy come through here on a pinto? Sorta dark-lookin'. Half Apache."

The smith shook his head. "There's another livery at the other side of town, though. He might put his horse there."

"Thanks. I'll have a look-see."

"You a bounty hunter?"

"No."

"You a—"

Raider turned to silence him with a stern look. The smithy smiled, a man who knew when to quit. He told Raider not to worry, he'd take good care of his mount. And the big man could sleep in the loft if he wanted.

Raider asked if he could store his gear in the loft. The smith said that would be fine, that he would guard the stuff with his life. Not to worry. He could even leave the Winchester up there if he wanted to.

"Why would I leave my rifle up there?" the big man asked.

"New marshal," the smith replied. "He's still allowin' men to wear their holsters, but he don't take to men carryin' rifles."

Raider pointed a finger at him. "If my Winchester is stolen, I'm takin' it outta your hide. Comprende?"

"No need to worry, stranger. It'll be safe with me. And you're welcome to sleep up there, just like I said."

Raider said he'd consider it.

He stored his gear in the loft and then climbed down into the stable again.

"Any place t' get a steak 'round here?" he asked.

"Miss Libby's Kitchen," the smith replied. "For six bits you can fill your belly."

Raider wore a look of amazement. "Six bits for a steak dinner?"

"Tombstone's a silver town, mister. Best get used to high prices."

The big man started for the door, calling over his shoulder, "I don't plan t' be 'round that long, honcho."

He had no idea how badly fate would prove him wrong.

• • •

Outside in the street, the town seemed almost peaceful. Evening had settled the wind. A low, orange haze hung over the town and the surrounding landscape. The air still smelled dusty, but it was better than getting pelted with specks of grit.

He strode toward the center of town, watching both sides of the street. Tombstone was calmer than he remembered it. No loud cowboys or prospectors on the street, no fights in alleys, no drunken miners staggering through the middle of town. He tried to recall any gaming or whoring establishments, the kinds of places that Johnny Blackfist might frequent.

Before he could reach the saloon, Raider caught sight of a bathhouse where an oil lamp was burning in the window. He stepped in to see a Chinese man hovering over a soapy tub. Raider asked if it was too late to get a bath and a shave. The man said no and that he could also have his clothes cleaned if he wanted. Six bits.

"Everything in this town cost six bits?" the big man asked.

The Chinaman just laughed. He called for a young woman, who took Raider's clothes when he was in the tub. She had long black hair and dark eyes that were half-hidden under heavy lids, a small body shifting under coarse fabric.

When she disappeared into the back, the Chinaman leaned over toward Raider, "You no lookee my daughter. You go cathouse like miners. Cost you six—"

"Yeah, I know, six bits." He considered it for a moment. "No thanks, pardner. Not t'night."

Not until he had captured Johnny Blackfist.

As he left Miss Libby's Kitchen, his belly full, Raider wondered what had happened since his last visit to Tombstone. The place was tame and lifeless, like a draft horse that had been pulling a wagon too long. If the town was going to be like this, then Johnny Blackfist wouldn't be too hard to find. He'd stand out like a gopher's head in a strawberry patch.

Raider pushed through the swinging doors of the barroom. Low oil lamps burned on the bar and on every table. The place wasn't crowded. Three men at the bar. One table of gamblers:

four cowboys and a dandified man in a suit. The dandy was dealing stud poker. Raider was tempted to join the game, but he decided to have a drink first.

The bartender poured him a shot of red-eye that Raider quickly knocked back. He asked for a refill. The bartender obliged him.

Raider glanced back toward the poker game. Nobody seemed to take any special notice of him. The dandy was dragging a big pile of chips toward him. Raider studied the profile, wondering if he had seen the dealer before. Reddish hair and moustache, rough face. As he was pulling his winnings toward his black silk vest, the dealer suddenly started coughing. He had to take a long tug from a whiskey bottle to make the cough subside. Then he spat into a can that he picked up from the floor.

"You want to play?" the bartender asked him.

Raider turned back to the bar. "No. You got any beer?"

"It's warm."

"Then give me two mugs full t' the top."

"Six bits for the beer and the red-eye," the bartender replied.

Raider had to laugh. "How'd I know that?"

"Beg pardon?"

"Nothin'."

Raider described Johnny Blackfist to the bartender, who had not seen anyone who matched the description.

"Lot of people through Tombstone these days," the man offered.

Raider squinted at him. "Don't seem busy t' me. Seems almost as quiet as Tucson or Phoenix."

"Not always," the barkeep replied. "But Marshal Earp has—"

Raider heard the commotion behind him. He turned again to look at the card table. Two men were rising. And just as quickly, there was gunfire, including the eruption of the big man's Colt.

CHAPTER FIVE

Allan Pinkerton leaned back in his chair, raising the coffee cup to his lips. He sipped the steaming liquid and looked out at the dim sky over Chicago. He felt satisfied, at least as much as a perfectionist like Pinkerton could feel satisfied. That stubborn, demanding streak in the Scotsman always rose to the surface. But on this particular night, he was feeling proud as he shared coffee with his assistant, William Wagner. "They're a good bunch of lads, William. Our boys are strong and true."

Wagner nodded, not sure if he felt comfortable with this sentimental side of his boss. "I do wish Raider could have been here, though. He, of all our men, needed to hear your lecture." He said it even though he didn't mean it.

Pinkerton grunted disapprovingly. "You had to go and mention him!"

Wagner realized he had made a mistake.

"It's bad enough that Stokes fell asleep, and now you mention the thorn in my side."

Wagner sighed. "Sorry I—"

"Not that I am displeased with Raider's results," Pinkerton

offered. "He just doesn't follow procedure. The day is coming when we won't need men like him and Stokes."

"You think the lawlessness will disappear?" Wagner asked, trying to divert the conversation away from the subject of Raider.

Pinkerton shook his head. "No, I don't. As great as this country is, there will always be black-hearted men who have no regard for the law. It's just—we'll need a different sort of man to fight corruption. A man who uses his guns only when he has to."

Wagner could not resist a little prodding that he might surely regret. "Well, Raider swears he only uses his gun when he has to."

"I know all about it," Pinkerton said. "He thinks he can kill every outlaw west of the Mississippi if we give him half a chance."

"He'd certainly try," Wagner agreed.

Pinkerton chuckled, shaking his head. "Where is the big oaf anyway?"

"Arizona."

Pinkerton nodded. "I remember now. Chasing that half-breed Apache. Have you heard from him lately?"

Wagner shook his head. "No. But I'm not worried. There's nothing else for him to do right now. Since I've sent everybody back into the field, we've covered all our bases."

Pinkerton nodded, sighing as he gazed out the window of his office. "Do you think the meeting was a success, William?"

Wagner nodded. "They're fine men, Allan. You can be proud of them. They'll build you a reputation that—"

Pinkerton glared at him. "Say it."

"A reputation that even Raider can't destroy."

"I hope you're right, William. I certainly hope you're right."

CHAPTER SIX

Raider had seen a lot of gunfights in his time, but few had ended as strangely as the one between the dealer and the card player.

It happened the same way most fights happen over cards. The player accused the dealer of cheating. The dealer denied it and told the player he should either learn how to play or give it up completely. The player's chair rattled as he stood and moved back, his hand dropping beside an old Army Colt on his hip.

"You've won every hand," the player accused. "I lost all my money. And I want it back."

Raider was surprised by the dealer's calm. The man remained still, his eyes locked on the player. As far as Raider could see, the dealer wasn't wearing any sidearms. Hard to tell, though, what he had hidden under his coat.

"Gimme my money," the player demanded.

The dealer gestured to the others, speaking in an icy voice, as if facing the Colt was an everyday occurrence. "Was I cheating, boys?"

They all shook their heads.

"No, Doc, you wasn't cheatin'."

"No, sir, Mister Holliday. You wasn't cheatin' at all."

"I didn't see no cheatin'."

The dealer smiled at the player, although it wasn't a warm expression. "You see. They don't think I was cheating."

The player swallowed hard, like he wasn't sure if he wanted to go through with his accusations. The dealer was ready to let him off the hook. Raider hoped it wouldn't come to gunplay, although the look in the player's eye said something about how important the money was to him. Maybe he had a wife at home, an old girl who would slam him on the head with a frying pan when he told her he had lost everything in a poker game.

Or maybe he just liked trouble.

"You been slippin' cards off'n the bottom of that deck since I came in here, Holliday. Now give me back my money."

The dealer tensed. "No," was his only reply.

The player's hand dropped toward his gun.

Raider froze, anticipating the report of the Colt.

The dealer moved so quickly that the big man was unaware of what happened next.

Clutching at his chest, the player staggered backward, slamming into the wall behind him. Blood poured from between his fingers. In the dim light, Raider could not see what had wounded him.

The dying man tried to lift his weapon but it went off inside the holster. He slumped to the floor, gasping for air. The dealer went around the table and bent over the body, trying to pull something from the man's chest. It was then that Raider saw movement on the other side of the barroom.

The dealer stood up, brandishing a bloodstained blade. "Anybody else think I was cheating?"

"You son of a bitch, you killed Jimmy."

The man across the barroom was aiming a Buntline straight at the dealer. The knife didn't stand a chance at such a range. Still, the dealer threw it even though it missed the mark.

Raider drew quickly and fanned the Colt three times. The Buntline man fell backward, squeezing the trigger but missing his target. He crashed into a table and rolled off onto the floor, twitching as he died.

The dealer gazed across the room at Raider.

The big man nodded, keeping his gun in hand to see if anybody else had an itchy trigger finger.

Behind him, the bartender peeked over the counter. "Is it finished?"

Raider sighed. "I reckon it is."

"Oh, Lordy," the bartender whined, "now Marshal Earp is gonna close me down for sure."

Raider watched as the gambler moved toward him. His hands were bloody from holding the knife. He came face to face with Raider and smiled again.

"Thanks."

Raider shrugged. "Didn't think it was fair for 'em t' gang up on you like that. An' he was too far away for the knife."

"That he was. Name's Holliday. Doc Holliday. I'd shake with you, but you see why I can't."

He held up his bloody hands.

"Doc, huh?"

Holliday grimaced. "You know me? You heard of me?"

"Cain't say as I have," Raider replied. "I just had me a pardner once name o' Doc. How come they call you that?"

"I used to be a dentist," Holliday replied. "Now I'm a gambler. You handle that gun pretty well. What line are you—?"

Everyone glanced toward the entrance as the swinging doors pushed open. A man in a black suit entered quickly with two other men behind him. The man wore a silver star on his lapel; wide-brimmed hat; shiny boots; three side arms, one on each hip and one in his belt. The men behind him carried shotguns.

Raider dropped his weapon back into his holster. "I'm figgerin' that's the new marshal everyone is talkin' 'bout."

"You figure right," Holliday replied. "Only he ain't that new."

Wyatt Earp stood still in the dim light, surveying the damage. Raider noted his face; grim expression, slack jaw and cheeks, thick black moustache, down-turned eyes, wrinkles like crow's feet. Earp either worried a lot, or drank a lot, or both.

He lifted his eyes, glaring toward the bar. "What happened?"

The bartender leaned over, pointing to the man who had been killed with the knife. "He claimed Doc Holliday was cheatin'. Then he tried to draw on him."

Earp tipped back the black Stetson. "Did this dead one draw first?"

Everybody agreed that he had.

Earp motioned to his men to carry out the body. He looked across the room at the other dead man. "What happened to him?"

"He tried to kill Doc after Doc defended himself," the bartender replied. "Then this stranger here drew and shot him down."

Earp strode slowly toward both men who leaned against the bar.

Holliday began to cough but quickly fought it back with another slug of whiskey. Raider just kept still, wondering how Earp was going to take to having a Pinkerton in town. Sometimes the local law boys got a little nervous when he entered their jurisdiction.

Earp came toe to toe with them. "What you got to say about all this, Doc? I want to hear it from you."

"What they claim is true," Holliday replied. "It happened exactly like they said. This big man here was just defending me and I was just defending myself. Nothing more or less."

Earp looked at Raider. "I'll have to ask for your gun, sir."

Raider frowned. "I ain't ready t' give it up, Marshal."

Everybody held their breath, watching as Raider and Earp stared each other down. Raider didn't want to kill a marshal, but he didn't want to surrender his Colt. He had already seen that Tombstone wasn't as tame as it seemed on the surface. Best to stay armed, even with the new marshal riding herd on things.

"A man kills another man in my town, I have to ask for his gun," Earp said. "You got truck with that?"

Raider shook his head. "Naw. But I got bus'ness here in Tombstone an' it's the kinda bus'ness where I'll need my Colt."

Earp took a deep breath, throwing back the tail of his coat so he could reach for the gun on his right hip.

Holliday laughed and clapped Earp on the shoulder.

"Wyatt, there's no call for that. Hell, this boy saved my life. Can't fault him for—"

He began to cough again, turning from them, reaching for the bottle on the counter.

Earp kept his gaze trained on Raider. "What kind of business you got here in Tombstone?"

Raider leaned in a little closer to the marshal. "Can you keep a secret, Earp? I'm a Pinkerton agent. Lookin' for a man name of Blackfist."

"Johnny Blackfist?" Earp asked eagerly.

Raider nodded. "You had trouble with him?"

"Plently. He—"

"Hey Wyatt!"

Earp turned to see that one of his deputies had come back into the bar. "What is it?"

"That dead one," the man replied. "He's one of the Musgrave brothers."

Earp pointed to the corpse that had not been removed yet. "See if that's the other Musgrave."

After a couple of moments, the body was identified as the second Musgrave brother. The deputy started to drag the corpse toward the door. The remaining barflies buzzed with whispers, making their way back to the bar.

Earp regarded Raider with his glassy eyes. "Well, I reckon I can't hold you responsible for killin' those Musgraves. Somebody would've done it sooner or later. They needed to be shot, only I could never rightly catch them at anything that warranted shooting."

Raider tipped his hat. "Glad t' be of help, Marshal. Mebbe you could return the favor. You seen Blackfist hereabouts?"

"No," Earp replied, "but if I see him first, you won't get a chance to capture him. I'll shoot him on sight."

"Just as long as he's stopped," Raider said.

Earp nodded and turned to walk away.

"Hey," Doc Holliday called, "you ain't gonna have a drink with us, Wyatt?"

Earp looked over his shoulder, glaring at Holliday. "I think you better go home, Doc. You've used up all your luck for one night."

Earp wheeled and headed out of the saloon.

Holliday grimaced, knocking back a slug from the bottle of

red-eye. "That sanctimonious, self-righteous—"

Raider wasn't sure, but he thought Holliday was cussing the marshal.

Holliday finally laughed. "Go home, he says. What home I got to go to? That fleabag hotel?"

Raider felt superior saying, "I'm stayin' at the stable myself."

"You're better off," Holliday replied. "Say, you ready for some tequila, Mister Pinkerton?"

"Easy," Raider urged. "I don't want that t' get 'round town too quick."

Holliday clapped him on the shoulder. "Aw, don't fret. You have nothing to worry about, leastways until Saturday night when all the yahoos come to town."

"Tombstone still seems pretty lawless t' me," Raider offered. "Even with Earp and those two deputies on duty."

Holliday laughed. "If Wyatt had his way, we'd all be sprouting angel wings. But that won't happen, partner."

"No, I reckon it won't."

"What do they call you?"

"Raider will do."

"Come on, Raider. Let's go have a drink."

The big man followed Doc out of the saloon.

CHAPTER SEVEN

Doc Holliday had a buggy sitting outside the saloon. As they climbed into the seat, a man came rushing through the swinging doors. He was holding a knife in his hand. Raider reached for his Colt until Holliday waved him off.

"No need, big man."

"Your knife, Mister Holliday," the man said, "you almost forgot it."

Holliday took the blade from the man and thanked him.

"I cleaned it for you just now," the man offered.

Holliday flipped him two bits and urged the buggy horse forward.

"Didn't see you pull that knife," Raider said.

Holliday held up his empty hands. "You didn't see me put it away just now either."

Raider chuckled appreciatively. "No, reckon I didn't."

The buggy rattled on into the night. They passed the edge of town and continued east on a bumpy road. When Raider asked where they were going, Holliday replied, "Some place where Wyatt's long arm ain't reached."

They rode for a long time in silence.

When Holliday slowed the wagon, Raider finally spoke up. "Funny, a man in your line o' work not carryin' a gun."

Holliday laughed and opened his hand to reveal a large caliber derringer. "I like to think of it as a pygmy rattler."

"Quick hands," the big man said. "Quick hands."

"I've also got a pocket revolver and a Diamondback on my person," the gambler rejoined. "And they both come out as quick as the knife."

"Diamondback, huh? Same as my old pardner."

Holliday nodded to a speck of light ahead of them on the trail. "A Mexican cantina, Raider. Have you ever been in such a place?"

"A time or two," the big man replied with a smile. "A time or two."

Raider thought Doc Holliday had outdone himself by taking them to the cantina. It was warm from a big hearth fire and the tequila tasted good, even if it did take the skin off the roof of a man's mouth. There were also two women named Rosita and Carmen who had devoted themselves to the pair of gringos who had been drinking most of the night.

Doc had inferred that Rosita, a round, thick-lipped girl with big breasts, could be had for the right price. Raider jokingly asked, "Six bits?" But the final tally was somewhat more. The big man told Rosita he would let her know if he needed her services.

"What's the matter, Raider?" Holliday asked. "I thought you'd be a man who appreciates the ladies."

"I am, Doc. I sure am. But I want another shot o' that tequila afore I do anythin' else."

Holliday raised his hand to the proprietor. "Pepe! Two more."

The Mexican man nodded. "Sí, señor."

"Happy to see us on a weeknight," Holliday said. "Pepe's business is slow until the weekend."

Raider dug into his pockets to see how much money he had left.

Holliday frowned at him. "Your money is no good tonight, Raider. Not after you saved my life. I owe you."

Raider nodded, still thinking that he had better request his back pay. "Is there a wire in Tombstone?" he asked.

Holliday nodded. "Didn't you see it when you rode in?"

"Cain't say as I did. But I'll take your word for it."

Holliday suddenly began to cough uncontrollably. He spat into a handkerchief and wiped his mouth. Another drink of tequila seemed to put him at ease.

"Consumption?" Raider asked.

"Dying from the inside out," Holliday replied with a nod. "But I won't let it stop me from living. Pepe?"

The proprietor of the cantina came toward them with a tray. "Señor, are you going to have the smoke tonight?"

Holliday nodded. The proprietor put the tray on the table. Raider saw the pipe and the brown weed that resembled tobacco. Loco weed, the big man thought. He wondered what it would do to the knife-wielding gentleman across the table from him.

The pipe glowed red in the dim light. Holliday puffed and offered the smoke to Raider, who declined. Holliday smoked again, leaning back in his chair. He seemed to relax, like the meanness went out of him.

"You and Earp," Raider said. "What's 'tween you two?"

Holliday glared sideways at him. "What do you mean?"

Raider shrugged. "He lets you gamble. He didn't run you in for killin' that man with your knife."

Holliday seemed to shift in the chair. Raider flinched when the knife hit the table, vibrating as the tip sank into the wood. The handle was carved bone and the thin blade seemed to be polished steel.

"I made it myself," Holliday said.

Raider nodded, thinking he had better be careful with the gambler. He could not remember when he had seen such speed in a man's fingers. No wonder Holliday didn't carry a holstered sidearm.

The gambler stared up at the ceiling. "I'm useful to Wyatt," he offered. "I can help him. Two men were killed tonight because of me."

"Thought you two was friends?"

Holliday laughed cynically. "Wyatt has no friends. The law. The law is the only friend of Mr. Earp. You see, the sooner he cleans out Tombstone, the sooner he makes a name for himself."

Raider shook his head back and forth. "Dang me if I cain't

figger out why I never heard of Earp. I mean, I've been operatin' in the north a lot lately, but seems I woulda heard somethin' 'bout him."

"If the Clanton gang keeps pushing him, you're going to hear plenty."

Raider suddenly felt like the company of the Mexican woman. "Where can we be alone with the señoritas, Doc?"

Holliday grinned. "Now you're talking, Raider." The gambler stood up and nodded to Pepe, who nodded back. "Just let me go free myself of some water and I'll show you the way to Rosita's bedroom."

Raider nodded assent.

Holliday disappeared out a side door.

Raider looked back down at the table. The knife was gone. Raider hadn't even seen Holliday take it. Quick hands. Too damned quick if he wanted to cross you. But Raider decided not to worry about it.

He glanced toward the Mexican woman who winked and smiled at him. Not bad. He wondered if she would smell like peppers.

A rustling as the front door opened.

"Hey, Doc," Raider said, "think this girl is—"

"Don't move, Pinkerton."

Raider turned to look at Johnny Blackfist, who stood in the door with his pistol drawn.

"So," Blackfist said, "you almost caught me in Pearce. But now I've caught you. And you will be the one to die."

Raider studied the angle. He would have to take a slug when he drew on the half-breed. If he rolled and fired at the same time, maybe the bullet would get him in the shoulder.

Blackfist raised the weapon to take careful aim. "Goodbye, Pinkerton. You won't chase me again. I—arr—"

Blackfist's body tensed. He staggered forward, the gun dropping from his gloved hand. When he fell on the floor, Raider saw the knife sticking out of his back.

Doc Holliday moved through the door, gazing down as the life ebbed from the outlaw's body. "See what I mean?" the gambler said. "I'm useful. This is the man you and Wyatt were talking about."

Raider exhaled. "Yeah, that's the one, Doc."

Holliday was glassy-eyed when he looked up. "Wyatt will probably want to take credit for this."

A shrug from the big Pinkerton. "Okay by me."

Holliday sat down again. "Maybe he was the one."

Raider squinted at the gambler. "What?"

"Maybe it's over."

"What's over?"

Suddenly Holliday began to cough again.

Raider pushed a mug of tequila toward him.

The gambler drank and the coughing subsided. "Dying from the inside out," he said, "but let's not let it ruin our fun. Come on, girls. We're ready for you."

Raider caught Holliday glancing sideways at him. "What is it, Doc?"

"After this," the gambler replied, "we're even, Pinkerton. An eye for an eye. Understand?"

Raider nodded and they shook on it.

Holliday began to cough again.

Raider took a deep breath, thinking he would be glad to get the hell out of Tombstone. The place really hadn't changed at all. If a man wasn't careful, he could still wind up six feet under, a permanent resident of Boot Hill.

CHAPTER EIGHT

Raider felt the warmth of the woman next to him. His face brushed her hair, filling him with the scent of her perfume. Without even opening his eyes, he pulled her close to him, rubbing his crotch against her plump backside. Rosita responded, rolling over, pressing her naked body into his.

"So beeg," were her waking words.

Raider did not bother to speak. Instead, he spread her thick thighs and settled in between her legs, prodding with his erect member. Rosita writhed under him in an attempt to help him enter.

"Slower," she whispered in his ear.

He tried to take it easy, but when the tip of his prick touched her moist cunt, he made one last thrust that sent him into her.

Rosita's head went back and she emitted a low groan from her open mouth. Her breasts shook as Raider began his up and down motion. She hung on, feeling his prick expand when his climax rose inside him.

Her body shook with his release.

Raider rolled off her, lying back on the feather mattress, trying to get his bearings.

Rosita snuggled close to him.

The big man stared up at the cracked plaster ceiling of one of the cantina's back rooms. It all came back to him, like a recalled dream. Doc Holliday, Johnny Blackfist, the knife in his back. Raider had to wonder if Marshal Earp would question the back wound. Probably not, not for a man like Blackfist. On one count, Raider had to admire the marshal; dead outlaws were less trouble than live ones. Earp didn't seem to mind planting a few bad men.

Raider climbed off the bed, gazing out the window. The heat told him that midday was close. He wondered if Holliday was still around. Then there was the body of Johnny Blackfist to consider. Messages to the home office were in order, along with the dreaded written report. And what if the territorial governor wanted Blackfist brought back to Tucson?

"Cowboy, get back in bed," Rosita demanded.

He waved her off. "Got bus'ness, woman. Maybe I'll be around t'night."

Her thick lips were drawn in a pout. "I will be with someone else."

He grinned as he reached for his pants. "You're breakin' my heart, honey."

She put her head back into the pillow, ignoring him.

Outside the window, harnesses rattled.

Raider glanced up to see Doc Holliday easing the buggy forward. "Hey, Raider," the gambler called. "Do you plan on sleeping all day?"

The big man was pulling on his shirt. "Hold on, Holliday. I'll be right along. By the way, where the hell is Blackfist?"

Holliday pointed to the rear of the buggy, where a large canvas bundle had been tied securely. "He's riding with us. Come on, we have to take him in to Wyatt. This will be a field day for the marshal."

Raider finished dressing and hurried to join Doc Holliday on the seat of the buggy. The day was so hot that the big man immediately broke into a sweat. His mouth grew drier as they rolled toward Tombstone.

"Jug of water under the seat," Holliday offered.

Raider thanked him and reached for the jug.

"Tequila will do that to you." the gambler commented.

Raider just nodded, taking several long drinks.

As they approached the dusty town, Raider saw Boot Hill in the distance. "I wonder if the marshal has those two boys in the ground by now?"

"The Musgraves? Hell, no."

Raider gawked at the gambler. "You sure 'bout that?"

"You don't know Wyatt, Raider. He'll play it for all it's worth. Especially when we get Blackfist to him. You'll see."

Raider was confused until they rode down the middle of Main Street. Then he saw the coffins on the porch, in front of marshal's office. Both caskets were open so everyone could see the pale gray death masks of the late Musgrave brothers. Above the coffins was a painted sign that read: "Outlaws are not welcome Tombstone. Marshal Wyatt Earp."

"Damn," the big man said with a grin.

"I told you," Doc Holliday rejoined. "Wyatt doesn't play."

Holliday went into the marshal's office and came back out immediately with Earp behind him.

The marshal's troubled faced gazed sorrowfully at the bundle in the back of the buggy. "I'll have one of the deputies get another coffin."

"They may want me t' take him back t' Tucson," Raider suggested. "After all, I was chasin' him for the gov'nor's office."

Earp glanced sharply at Raider. "I enforce the laws of this territory. Do you understand that?"

Raider nodded. "But I still have t' send messages t' Phoenix an' Tucson, t' let the people who hired me know that Blackfist is dead."

Earp brushed back his coattail to reveal the new Buntline he was wearing on his right hip. Taken from the dead Musgrave brother, Raider thought. He wondered if he would ever have to face Earp in a standoff.

"Do what you have to do," Earp said. "But Blackfist is going to Boot Hill with these other two."

Raider shrugged. "No offense taken, Marshal. It don't matter t' me where you plant him, as long as he's planted." Raider could not resist a disrespectful wink at the lawman.

Earp seemed to bristle.

Doc Holliday stepped between them. "Come on, Raider. Let's get some food in us."

The big man stepped down from the buggy, thinking that Wyatt Earp was like most lawmen he met. The marshal definitely had a burr under his saddle. No matter how hard he tried, the tall Pinkerton from Arkansas could not show much respect for the local lawman, even if Earp was some hot shot gunman who seemed bent on building a reputation.

Holliday urged Raider toward Miss Libby's Kitchen. "Wyatt doesn't appreciate your wit, Raider."

"Yeah, he seems a little tight-assed, don't he?"

"He is, friend. And more than a little."

They crossed the street only to find that the restaurant was not open. But Doc Holliday sweet-talked Miss Libby into providing them with some beef stew and homemade bread. Raider had two helpings of the stew and then used the bread to sop up the gravy.

When they were finished, Raider leaned back in his chair. "Well, I reckon I got work t' do."

"Yeah?" Holliday said. "Like what?"

Raider shrugged. "Gotta send wires an' write my report. Ask for my back pay, get my next assignment."

"There's a lot more to being a Pinkerton than meets the eye."

"Sometimes it can be downright bothersome," Raider replied; "but I reckon I ain't good at much else."

"I've always thought a man takes naturally to his own line of work," Holliday offered. "That's why I became a gambler."

"Thought you were a tooth-yanker."

Holliday grinned. "Got tired of that. No, I'm a born gambler. That's why I like it so much here in Tombstone. The dice are always rolling."

"Never cared much for dice myself."

Holliday raised an eyebrow. "How about poker? You like poker?"

"Usually I do," the big man replied, "but—"

"Don't be shy."

Raider exhaled. "Well, I just don't think Tombstone's the kinda place where you wanna push your luck."

Holliday grinned and nodded.

• • •

As they left Miss Libby's, they saw Wyatt Earp on the porch of his office, giving a speech to several townsfolk who had gathered to view the bodies.

"Our nightmare is over," he said to them. "As your marshal, I promise that one day Tombstone will be a place to raise your children, to grow old and see your grandchildren."

Holliday looked at Raider, grinning. "He never stops."

Raider tipped his hat to the gambler. "See you in the saloon t'night, Doc. Maybe I'll play a few hands with you."

"I guarantee that I don't cheat, Raider. Most men are gutless or too bold. But I'm right in the middle. I play each hand for what it's worth. No more, no less."

They shook hands.

Holliday headed for the hotel.

Raider looked back at Wyatt Earp. The lawman was rattling on about truth and justice, two things that didn't necessarily go together as far as Raider could see. He regarded Earp, wondering what it was about the lawman that made him so uneasy. Maybe it was the strange glow in Earp's glassy eyes. A man who didn't sleep, a man who worried a lot. A man who didn't mind killing as long as it made him look good. Raider wasn't sure he trusted Earp, even if they did see eye to eye on a few things.

He shook off the odd feelings and walked over to the wire office.

His first two messages were to the men who had hired him to find Blackfist. Both communiqués read: "Blackfist dead. Tombstone marshal wants to bury him here. Is that all right?" He told the operator to send the telegrams so that the men on the other end of the line could pay the charges.

Since he had a feeling that Blackfist would not be wanted back in Tucson or Phoenix, he decided to inform the home office that he was finished and ready for a new assignment. He also requested any back pay that he had coming to him, as his pockets were nearly empty. Five dollars left to his name. Some men might have found the sum to be adequate, but not a man with Raider's habits. Women and whiskey would put a dent in five dollars in a hurry, and gambling would make it disappear even more quickly.

Nothing to do but head back to the stable and check on his belongings. He told the key operator to bring any messages for him to the livery. He'd be sleeping in the loft until his back pay arrived.

When he went out into the street again, he glanced toward the marshal's office. Earp was no longer there on the porch, but a few spectators were viewing the corpses. Raider had to admit to himself that Earp had the right idea for law enforcement. Show the criminals what would happen if they crossed him in his town. Maybe Tombstone was on its way to being a lawful community.

Back at the stable, the livery man assured Raider that his belongings had not been touched. Sure enough, his gear was safe and sound in the loft. Raider leaned back on his saddle, closing his eyes, resting until the telegraph man came by near the end of the day.

He had two messages for Raider. One said that the territorial government entrusted Marshal Earp with the burial of Johnny Blackfist and that any reward was to go to the marshal's office. The other telegram was from the home office, instructing Raider to sit tight in Tombstone until his next assignment came through. There was also thirty dollars in back pay.

Raider tossed the operator two bits and returned to the loft. He welcomed the back pay and the fact that he did not have to take Blackfist's body to Tucson. But staying in Tombstone was another matter. How long would Wagner make him wait in the dusty town?

"You okay up there?" the livery man called from below.

Raider said he was fine. But he didn't feel fine. He only felt a sense of dread that sometimes preceded bad things.

Maybe he should just leave Tombstone, head for the nearest town that had a wire, inform Wagner that he could be reached there.

Of course, Wagner would be put out because Raider had not followed orders. But what the hell could Wagner do? Fire him?

Raider leaned back on the saddle again. His head was still foggy from the night in the cantina. He would have to stay away from there as long as he was in Tombstone. Best just to lay low, keep out of trouble.

He tried to sleep but found that his eyes would not close for more than a couple of minutes.

So he rose and sat by the window, watching the street. Just at dusk, a group of four horsemen rode slowly down the main street. They were clad in dusters, carrying sidearms and rifles on the sling rings of their saddles. When they saw the caskets in front of the marshal's office, they reined up and stared at the dead bodies.

Wyatt Earp came out to face them from the porch.

No words passed, but an ugly man at the front of the group spat when he saw Earp. The marshal tensed, lowering his hand toward the Buntline. But the men on horseback did not want a showdown, so they rode slowly toward the edge of town. Earp watched for a while and then went back into his office.

Raider climbed down the ladder to see the smith at his anvil. "Those men who just passed. Who were they?"

"The Clantons," the smith replied. "They hate Earp and he hates them."

"Why ain't they shot it out yet?"

The smith shrugged. "I reckon both sides is waitin' for the right chance. If it comes to that."

Raider figured it was something he wanted to avoid at all costs. Best to stay out of other people's troubles. No sense in getting killed over a truck that wasn't your own.

"I'm gettin' hungry," the big man said.

"Miss Libby has a special on fried chicken tonight."

Raider took a couple of silver dollars from his pocket. "How 'bout I treat you t' dinner if you'll go git it?"

The smith wiped his forehead. "Never have been one to turn down a free meal. Course, if I'm goin' to get it, then it ain't exactly free."

Raider flipped him another six bits. "Git some beer, too. Mebbe a bottle if you can find one cheap 'nough."

The smith took off his apron and hurried to his task.

Raider figured to play it safe the rest of the way. Just fill his belly, lay low in the loft, wait patiently until his next assignment came in over the wire. No sense tempting fate; not if he didn't have to. Just get a good night's rest and leave town if the wire didn't come in a couple of days. He didn't consider that trouble might try to find him in the middle of the night.

• • •

He heard screams before he heard the gunshots.

Raider raised up, listening. He had been sound asleep until the screams had echoed in the darkness. He wondered if he had been dreaming. Maybe it was part of some nightmare.

Someone moaned. The sound was more muffled than the screams. Raider thought for a moment that he was hearing the reverberating cries of a man and a woman making love. Then he heard coughing.

Was Doc Holliday in trouble?

The cough didn't sound as bad as the gambler's.

"Please—no—"

It was somebody in trouble. But where? Noises could echo over rooftops in a town and you would never find the direction.

He heard a dull thud.

Another high-pitched scream, quickly muffled.

Raider reached for his Colt. It sounded like it was coming from behind the livery. He knew that was the first place he wanted to look.

The horses snorted as he came down the ladder. He made his way through the shadows toward the back door. The latch was easy to work, even in the dark with the Colt in one hand. The hinges creaked as he pushed the door open.

Cool night air rushed over him. He heard another dull thud, detected the whining cry of desperation on the breeze. Was that another voice coming behind the one in pain?

He stepped slowly through the threshold, inching down the dark alley. What if Earp saw him with the Colt drawn? The marshal might try to cut Raider in half with the Buntline. Although Raider really couldn't say that he had seen Earp shoot anybody—yet.

"No—please—no more—"

The second voice muttered incoherently. Too weak to carry far. Maybe they were close by.

Raider moved through the back alley until he heard the second voice more clearly. The words came in bits in pieces. "Thought you could escape—justice—retribution—" Was that dull laughter?

The big man wiped his forehead with the back of his hand. He had to find them, to see for himself. What the hell was going on in the middle of the night in Tombstone?

A loud crack reached him in the stillness. It sounded like steel breaking bone. He began to run toward the noise when he heard it again. More muffled cries. Then the second voice: "Shut up, shut up—"

Raider heard them moving in the shadows. He thought he saw fluttering shapes in a hay shed. Then the loud crack came again, followed by whimpering.

He wheeled toward the shed, pointing the Colt at the shadows. "Don't move, whoever you are. Stay real still and—"

A gun went off, showering the hay shed with a momentary flash of red sparks. Raider saw the two figures. One of them seemed to be tied up against the wall of the shed. And the man with the pistol had shot him.

Raider fired twice but the gunman was already running. He turned a corner and seemed to disappear into the night. Raider followed, running through the alley until he tripped and slammed onto the ground.

Leaping back to his feet, he hesitated, listening for the scuffling feet of the fleeing gunman. Nothing. Maybe the pistolero had rounded the corner and stopped to wait for Raider. It wasn't a bad trick since it would give him the drop on his pursuer. Raider had gotten away with it a couple of times himself.

So instead of streaking around the corner in pursuit, Raider gave a wide, slow turn. Somebody was waiting for him. He flinched when the two shots rang out again. Slugs whizzed by his head, slamming into the building behind him. Raider replied with two more shots of his own, firing at the muzzle flash of the ambusher.

The dark figure ran again. Raider fired but the shots did not seem to hit their mark. The alley was dark and narrow. Nothing to do but run after the man and hope he could catch him.

But Raider never caught up with the fleeing shadow. He broke out of the alley just in time to hear a horse galloping away from town. He emptied his Colt into the darkness, listening to see if he had hit anything. But the horse just kept running, leaving Tombstone in a hurry.

"Damn—"

He remembered the victim in the hay shed.

As quickly as his legs would carry him, he made his way

through the alley. It took him a few minutes to find the hay
shed. He had almost gotten lost in pursuit of the gunman.

"You hear me?" he said as he approached the shed.

No reply.

He drew closer to the man who was hanging on the wall of
the shed.

"Hey? You still with us?"

He dug into his shirt pocket, reaching for a match. Nothing
there. He'd have to go back to the stable to get a lantern.

As he turned, a rifle lever chortled in the cool night air.

"Hold it right there, Pinkerton!"

Raider squinted as a mining lamp swelled with orange
light. He could see three men moving toward him. One wore a
badge on the lapel of his coat.

"Marshal Earp!"

Wyatt Earp gestured with the barrel of a Winchester. "Get
his gun. And be careful."

Raider froze. "Hey, wait a minute. You ain't—"

Earp looked down the barrel of the rifle. "Give up that gun
or I'll drop you in a second."

"You got it all wrong, Earp—"

But Raider dropped his Colt.

"I didn't do anythin'!" he insisted.

"You're under arrest," Earp told him.

Raider scowled at the lawman. "For what?"

Earp nodded toward the man who was hanging dead on the
back of the hay shed. "For that."

One of the deputies raised the lantern so Raider could see
what the gunman had left behind.

When Raider beheld the gruesome spectacle, he had to
fight to keep from emptying his guts right there in front of the
lawmen.

know an awful lot about what happened here, Pinkerton. That leads me to believe you were the one who killed this man."

"God almighty, Earp, gimme some credit for havin' a few brains. If I was gonna torture somebody t' death, why would I do it right here under your nose? Why would I run wild asses all over Tombstone, blastin' away in the middle o' the night?"

"He has a point, Wyatt."

Earp silenced his man with a harsh glance.

"Come on," Raider offered. "Lemme show you where I chased him. There oughta be some signs o' where he shot at me."

Earp considered for a moment and then nodded. "But you have to let us tie your hands first."

Raider agreed, as long as he was allowed to show them the evidence.

When his hands were bound in front of him, he started down the alley with the deputy carrying the lamp. The big man had to consider what he would do if Earp didn't believe him. An escape attempt might be in order if Earp insisted on locking him up. But first things first. He needed to find the bullet holes that had been caused by the murderer's pistol.

They searched the rotting walls of the building until they saw the splintered clapboards. The slugs were six feet off the ground. Raider figured he must have ducked instinctively, otherwise the bullets would have creased his skull.

"They look fresh," said the deputy with the lantern.

Raider urged them to dig the slugs out of the wood. The deputy used a pocket knife to retrieve the chunks of lead. Raider asked him to hold the slugs in the light.

"Look," he told Earp, "the gun that fired these slugs is smaller than mine. Prob'ly a .38 or a .36 caliber."

Earp seemed to be taking it all in, his expression never changing. He told one of his men to check farther down the alley, to see if he could find anything else. The man took the lantern and started off.

Earp stared at Raider in the darkness. "All right, Pinkerton. You seem to have figured all this out in a hurry—"

"Just looked at what I saw," Raider offered.

"I'm sure." Earp cleared his throat. "Suppose you tell me why that man was killed in the first place?"

Raider scowled at the lawman. "Hey, I ain't been on this

case that long. How the hell am I s'posed t' know?"

Earp shook his head. "And I thought it was all over after Blackfist died."

"Come again?" the big man asked.

"Wyatt!"

They glanced down the alley to see the deputy waving the lantern.

Earp put the rifle bore in Raider's back. "You first."

They moved slowly toward the swinging lantern.

"Blood," the deputy said. "And it's fresh."

Raider studied the clotting blob of red. "I must've hit him after all. Damn, it just grazed him though."

Earp cast a puzzled look at the big Pinkerton. "What makes you say that?"

Raider shrugged. "He still had enough strength t' git away. Prob'ly hit an arm or a leg."

Earp rubbed his chin again, like he wasn't sure about anything.

Raider nodded toward the end of the alley, where it broke open into clear land. "If you check down there, you'll find where he tied his horse."

Earp looked skeptical, but he still ordered everyone to the end of the alley. Sure enough, they found fresh hoofprints and a pile of steaming manure. Raider beamed proudly, wondering what Earp was going to say about his expertise as a detective.

The marshal glared at him. "What do you say about this?"

Raider used his bound hands to push back his Stetson. "Well, the horse was here for a while. It had 'nough time t' shit."

One of the deputies laughed.

Earp silenced him with another stern look. "Why was the horse tied here so long?" he asked Raider.

The big man closed his eyes, thinking about the things he had heard minutes before. "Somebody was chasin' the man who was killed," he said finally. "The man got away from the bushwhacker and the bushwhacker had t' chase him down. He left his horse here while he searched."

"Aw, that don't make sense," one of the deputies offered.

"Let him talk," Earp said. "Go on."

"It's like I said afore," Raider offered. "If you was gonna commit this kind o' killin', would you do it in the middle o'

Tombstone? You wouldn't. You'd torture the man someplace where nobody could hear you. You wouldn't nail him up—"

One of the deputies turned away to puke.

Raider shook his head, exhaling. "I know just what you mean, pardner. But we gotta look at what really happened. My guess is, that dead one escaped from his tormenter. The bushwhacker came after him an' caught him in this alley. You can see what happened next."

Earp paced back and forth for a few steps, then pointed a finger at the big man. "You say the killer caught him. Why didn't he take him back to where he was in the first place?"

"Figgered t' finish him quick," Raider replied. "Only he wasn't figgerin' on me bein' there."

Earp shook his head. "You coulda planned the whole thing. Put the horse there. You had somebody workin' with you. You both fired all those shots and then your pard rode away. You weren't countin' on me and my men comin' after you. But we caught you in the act."

"It ain't like that, Earp."

"No? Why ain't it? You claim to have shot at the killer, but you missed him. Yet, in the saloon, which is almost as dark as the alley, you managed to kill one of the Musgrave brothers without too much trouble."

"Yeah!" the deputy rejoined.

Raider exhaled defeatedly. "Yeah, that's it, Earp. I'm a dumb son of a bitch who'd ride into the roughest town in Arizona, t' commit a murder in the jurisdiction of the toughest marshal I ever saw. I'm so stupid that I ran all over the place, shootin' and whoopin' it up, makin' enough noise t' raise the friggin' dead. I'm so damned brainless that I'd stand here an' try t' make up this bullshit story so—"

"That's enough," Earp said.

"No," Raider replied, "it ain't nearly enough. 'Cause if you lock me up, I'll send a message t' the agency an' your town'll be crawlin' with Pinks who are lookin' for the truth. Even if you hang me, they won't leave you alone."

Earp's eyes narrowed. "Take him back to the hay shed."

Raider had to go with them. They had the guns. When they were looking at the body again, Earp asked Raider to tell him what he saw.

Even though Raider was steamed, he still managed to survey the carnage in the dim light of the lantern. "Damn."

Earp bristled. "What now?"

"Somebody hated this man. Look at what they done to him. Some o' those marks on his face are scorpion bites. Like somebody put a scorpion on his face."

One of the deputies groaned again.

Raider motioned to the man with the lantern. "Gimme that light."

He grabbed the lantern with his bound hands and held it up closer to the dead man. "Jesus save us all. His face is so bad that we couldn't tell who he was even if we knew him. And that hatchet was used on his knees. Look here. Somebody was whippin' him."

"What I feared," Earp said. "Just like the others."

Raider glared at the lawman. "Others?"

"What else?" Earp insisted.

Raider went back to studying the victim. "Well, he weren't old, but he weren't young. Look there. Gray hairs. He musta been strong, though. Looks like they was workin' on him a long time. God. Why the hell did the killer have t' nail him up?"

"A crucifixion," Earp said. "Used by the Romans as punishment. The way they killed Jesus."

Raider wasn't sure what to say after that remark.

One of the deputies took the lantern away from him. "Want us to call the undertaker, Marshal?"

Earp looked at Raider. "Unless our friend here wants to examine the body closer. What you say, Pinkerton?"

"I seen enough. Unless—"

"Go on," Earp said.

"Well, he's wearin' a pair o' pants"— That was all the dead man wore— "mebbe you could check the pockets."

The deputy with the lantern made a gagging noise. "You're a sick son of a bitch, Pinkerton."

"No he's not," Earp replied. "But we'll have the undertaker bring the dead man's pants to us when he's finished."

"Good idea," Raider said. He held out his hands. "How 'bout untyin' me, Earp?"

The marshal shook his head. "I can't. Not until I've seen your papers. And even then, I'll have to lock you up for a while."

Raider frowned. "But—"

"No buts, Pinkerton. You do like I say and you may live a while longer. Understand?"

Raider could only nod agreement. He had to cooperate—at least while they had all the guns.

The Tombstone jail was cleaner than most of the other lockups that Raider had seen in his time. Nothing fancy, just a sturdy rope and board bed with a corn shuck mattress. Water bucket and slop jar. And bars. Gray iron bars that held a man in captivity. Too many bars. And a door that clinked shut with the lonesomest sound known to anyone who had heard it from the inside.

"Am I gonna hang?" Raider asked as Earp turned the key.

The marshal did not reply.

"I want somebody who knows how t' thump a law book!" Raider cried as the marshal turned to leave. "I know somethin' of the law. I know it's on my side till you prove diff'rent!"

Earp did not seem interested.

Nothing to do but lay back on the cot, relax, try to think.

Raider wondered if Earp believed him. The marshal's reaction didn't seem like anything to bank on. Raider could not let himself believe that someone so interested in justice would hang an innocent man.

Then again, Earp had shown a tendency toward acting the big shot, playing things out. The display of dead outlaws, however much it worked, was not the act of a typical lawman. Earp seemed to have other things on his mind. What if he felt like throwing a fallen Pinkerton into the rattlesnake pit? Raider was the perfect sacrifice, a scapegoat for the horrible killing.

Raider felt his stomach turning. His own troubles slid downstream when he thought about the poor bastard he had found strung up in the hay shed. He had seen men in bad shape before, but never one that gave him such a rotten sensation all over his body. He felt dirty, like he had seen something no man was meant to see, a glimpse of a beast that he had not encountered in a long time.

Forcing himself to recall the details, he pieced together a few things. Most of what he had told Earp was off the top of his head. But looking back, it seemed to make sense. The victim had escaped after torture, only to have the killer catch up to him. Then the victim had been finished off in the back alley. The murderer probably hadn't intended to leave the corpse in town, but a certain trouble-finding Pinkerton had been awakened by the noise.

He tried to remember the voices he had heard in the alley. What was it the killer had said? Retribution. Maybe the victim had deserved his fate. Maybe the killer had just been paying him back for past transgressions.

Raider shook his head, trying to fight off the chill that raced up and down his backbone. No man deserved to die like a pig on a butcher's hook. Even if the victim had committed some terrible crime, at least he should have the right to die on the end of a rope, paying the hangman to tie a good knot.

He tossed and turned on the cot until the sky outside began to change into a dull, bluish tint. Morning was already there. No way to sleep after he had seen that dead man. So he sat on the edge of the cot and watched through the bars until the sun appeared overhead.

The door opened between the cell and Earp's office.

"You hungry, Raider?" Doc Holliday stuck his head through the doorway.

Raider smiled sheepishly. "Earp gonna lock you up too, Doc?"

Holliday came toward the cell, carrying a tray. "Got a real Arizona home-cooked breakfast here, Raider. Five eggs, steak, biscuits, gravy, potatoes, sweet peppers, salsa relish, and bacon."

Raider waved him off. "Ain't hungry."

"Grits, too," Holliday offered.

Raider smelled the food and suddenly wanted to eat.

Holliday slid the tray under the door and watched him as he ate. "I knew an old son of Dixie like you couldn't turn down grits."

"Mind if I use your knife t' cut this steak, Doc?"

Holliday grinned appreciatively. "Nice try, Pinkerton. But the blade stays at home. I—"

"Doc!" Wyatt Earp looked through the doorway. "Doc, I want you to do something for me. In a hurry."

"Be right there, Wyatt." Holliday winked at Raider. "Don't worry, boy. I'll have you out in a jiffy."

Raider glanced up. "No lie?"

"Either that or I'll start tying thirteen loops on your neck-knot."

Holliday laughed but Raider wasn't sure if he was joshing him.

He finished his breakfast, wondering if it was his last meal.

CHAPTER TEN

William Wagner usually walked to the Pinkerton agency every morning. He didn't live far away and he was too thrifty to spend money on a coach. It wouldn't have looked good to the other men who worked in the office if he arrived in a fancy carriage to begin his duties every day.

Even during the winter, when the snow blew through the air like dandelion fluff, he still bundled up and trod briskly to the office. Once or twice he had been stopped by blizzard conditions, but usually he managed to make it up Fifth Avenue to the warm rooms of the well-known agency. Sometimes shopkeepers checked their clocks by Wagner's passing.

On this particular sunny morning, Wagner ambled along Fifth Avenue, hardly expecting to be approached by a huffing messenger boy from the Western Union office. The lad had broken a sweat and seemed fatigued, although he had just begun his day. He almost bowled Wagner over trying to catch up with him.

"Sir," he panted, trying to catch his breath. "This came. I was on the way when—I saw you—"

He thrust a telegram at Wagner.

"See here, my young fellow, couldn't this have waited until I was at my desk? I was rather hoping to enjoy the rest of my walk!"

But the messenger boy was undaunted by Wagner's commanding tone. "Read it now, sir. It's about Raider."

Wagner angrily snatched the paper from the lad's hand. "Raider indeed. I've a mind to—" He began to read the telegram.

The boy waited anxiously, watching for Wagner's response.

"Good Lord!" the gentleman cried.

"See," the boy rejoined. "I told you it was big. How about that? The marshal Wyatt Earp himself."

Wagner cast a wary glance at the lad. "I appreciate your stopping me, boy, but shouldn't you be running along?"

"Er, yes, sir."

When he hesitated, Wagner tossed the boy a nickle. "Now run a long."

"Thank you, Mr. Wagner. Thank you very much."

Wagner forgot the intrusion, making for the office with the telegram in hand. He was hoping Pinkerton had come in early, as was his custom. But since Wagner wanted him to be there, naturally the Scotsman had not arrived.

Pacing back and forth, Wagner watched the front door until his boss entered the agency.

Pinkerton saw the anxious look on Wagner's face. "So, William, have we an emergency already this morning?"

"Of sorts," Wagner replied, handing him the telegram.

Pinkerton read it and motioned for Wagner to follow him into his private office. "It didn't take Raider long to find trouble in Tombstone," he said as he sat down behind his desk.

Wagner nodded, looking at the floor. "No, sir. It's my fault. I shouldn't have made him stay there."

"Would it have mattered?" Pinkerton asked. "He might have gotten in trouble at the pearly gates of Heaven. And he probably will when he gets up there. Although with Raider, he'll most likely be at the devil's door."

"Yes, sir."

Pinkerton read the telegram again. "You know what to do, William."

"I'll send the reply immediately."

He left to pen the message to Tombstone.

Pinkerton leaned back in his chair, thinking that he had better make a cup of coffee for himself. It was probably going to be a long day. Messages about Raider so early in the morning could not be construed as good omens.

He just hoped the big galoot could find his way out of this one all by himself.

CHAPTER ELEVEN

The warm Arizona morning stretched into a hotter afternoon. Raider lay on the rope bed, considering his fate. Sweat broke over his face and body when the rapping of hammers on nailheads resounded outside the barred window. He rose to the casement, trying to see if a gallows was being erected in his honor. But he could only catch a view of the alley behind the Tombstone jailhouse.

He tried lying back on the mattress but suddenly it was too hot inside the plaster cell. Pacing didn't help. He sat on the edge of the bed, drenched in perspiration. He had been in tight spots before, but somehow he felt that this one might end with a rope around his neck.

Would Earp really do it? String him up for the townsfolk to see? He flinched when he heard something that resembled the rattling drop of a gallows trapdoor.

"Nervous, Pinkerton?"

Doc Holliday had come into the cell room from Earp's office.

Raider wiped his forehead with the back of his hand. "I forgot how hot it can git in Arizona."

Holliday grinned. "You won't have to worry about it too much longer."

Raider turned to study the gambler's face. "You look like you know somethin' I don't."

Holliday shrugged. "Maybe."

The gambler used his sleight-of-hand to produce a thick, new rope.

Raider frowned as Holliday's hands began to work on the noose. "That ain't funny, Doc."

Holliday quickly fashioned a hangman's knot. "Thirteen loops," he said, still smiling. "Unlucky for the one who wears it."

"I ain't ready for hangin'. Not yet, anyway."

But the gambler wasn't ready to give up tormenting the big man from Arkansas. He slipped the noose over his own neck and pulled it tight. His face turned a little red, but he still wore a shit-eating grin.

"You ain't funny," Raider offered, looking away.

Holliday ignored him. "You see, Raider, you have to get the hangman to lay the knot alongside your head. See, like this."

He demonstrated how the knot should be positioned, something that Raider already knew from his attendance at several hangings, not to mention a few that had been intended for him. He had always managed to escape at the last minute, however. He wondered if he would be as lucky this time.

"You don't want the knot in front or in back," Holliday went on. "If the knot is in back or in front, your neck won't break when you drop. No, instead, you'll strangle, slow-like, kicking and thrashing."

Raider stood up, facing the window. "I know all 'bout it, Holliday. I seen a hangin' or two in my time."

"No, you want the knot on the side," the gambler continued. "That way your neck breaks—snap—like a twig. You still thrash and kick, but you're dead so you don't feel it. Of course, some say that hanged men often display—how shall I put it—a hard Johnson."

"Well," the big man offered, "that's somethin' t' look forward to. If I haveta go out, I guess it's better t' go out angry."

They were both quiet for a while.

Holliday listened to the hammering and banging outside.

"Gonna have to build a big gallows for you, Raider. I mean, if a tall man like you dropped through, your feet might hit the ground and—"

"Will you shut your yap, Holliday!"

"Just funning," the gambler replied. "I figured you might want to have a few laughs before you go."

Raider wheeled around and sat on the edge of the bed again. "I ain't so all-fired ready t' go."

"Oh no?"

The big man grunted, leaning back against the wall. "They got a thing called the law in this country. They cain't string me up till I had a fair trial by a jury. Law of the land."

Holliday shrugged. "Maybe. Maybe not. Wyatt Earp is the law in Tombstone. Sometimes he acts as judge and jury. And the townsfolk don't care as long as he tries to bring peace to their little hamlet."

"I don't care what the citizens want," Raider replied. "I know the law of these U-nited States and the last time I checked, a man couldn't be hanged till he had a fair trial."

Holliday laughed. "That's all well and good. When you're in the States. But the last time I checked, Arizona was still a territory. The laws are different here."

Raider sat up, his face turning bright red. "Shit! I forgot 'bout that. But hell, they still have a terr'torial judge in these parts. I at least git t' say my piece in front o' him."

"Maybe. Maybe not. In case you didn't notice, Wyatt is something of a stumper. If he decides to sacrifice you in the name of justice, it won't matter if you say your piece or not."

Raider touched his neck. "Aw, kiss my ass, Holliday."

"Yeah, it's a shame," the gambler went on. "I was starting to like you, Raider. It's not often that I meet a man who shares my taste for the finer things in life. Good whiskey, cards, women. No. The way this territory is going, why, everyone will be respectable in a couple of years. A man will have to go Mexican to find—"

Holliday began to cough. He hacked for a long time, finally spitting blood into a handkerchief. Raider felt a little sorry for the gambler, even if he had been tormenting him. Holliday pulled a whiskey flask from his back pocket and took a long swallow to make the coughing stop.

Raider still couldn't resist digging at the gambler. "Hell,

Doc, the way you're goin', you may not live t' see me swing."

Holliday wheezed. "You could be right."

Raider got up, coming to the bars, holding on to the iron that was still cold in the heat of midday. "Tell me the truth, Holliday. You think I murdered that poor soul we found in the alley?"

Holliday shook his head. "No. But what I think doesn't matter. It's Wyatt that calls the shots in this town. He's the one who has to be convinced. And I'm not so sure that he—"

Something rattled behind the gambler, prompting him to turn around.

Wyatt Earp appeared in the doorway, holding a ring of keys.

"Hangin' time," said Doc Holliday.

Earp frowned at him. "No need for that kind of talk, Doc."

Raider felt a chill running from the iron bars into his body.

Earp handed Holliday the keys. "Let him out. And bring him into the front office."

Raider watched with hope as the gambler slipped the key into the hole of the cell door. Maybe this was the big man's chance to escape. If he could get a grip on Holliday, maybe take the gambler's knife— Of course, he would have to get through the marshal's office using Holliday as a shield. What if Earp had no compunctions about shooting both of them?

The iron door swung open.

Holliday stepped back, as if he had read the scheme in Raider's black eyes. "You first, Pinkerton. I don't want you sneaking up behind me."

Raider came out of the cell, measuring the distance to Holliday's thin neck. He wondered if the gambler would get the knife into him before he could kill him with his bare hands. Holliday kept backing off, like he knew what Raider had in mind.

"Easy," the gambler warned. "Don't make Wyatt shoot you. He'd hate to cheat the hangman."

Holliday ushered Raider into Earp's office. It wasn't much. A battered oak desk and a couple of chairs. Behind the desk hung a commendation from the Kansas City police department. Raider tried to remember the times he had worked with the Kansas City constabulary. Had he run into Earp before?

The marshal sat behind his desk, rubbing his eyes with his hands.

Holliday motioned toward the framed commendation. "Yessiree, ol' Wyatt here used to be a hotshot with the Kansas City coppers. But that wasn't wild enough for him so he struck out for the west. Now he's—"

Earp glared at the gambler. "That will be enough out of you, Doc."

Raider studied the distance to the door. If he could get out, steal a horse, ride to freedom— Best to get away if he could. The business in Tombstone no longer interested him, not if he had to hang for it.

Holliday frowned at the marshal. "Aw, Wyatt, you don't have to talk to me like that. I was just trying to amuse our guest."

Raider snorted. "Yeah, I'm sure as hell amused. Don't put yourself out for me, hell, you can even stop work on that gallows an' I won't have any hard feelin's."

Earp's pale brow wrinkled. "Gallows?"

Raider pointed toward the window. "All that hammerin' and nailin'. Ain't they buildin' a platform t' string me up?"

"No," Earp replied. "They're puttin' a roof on the place next door."

Holliday started edging toward the door. "I'll just be on my way—"

Raider moved to grab the gambler. "You son of a—"

Earp stood up, drawing the Buntline from his holster. "No need for that, Pinkerton."

Holliday held up the hangman's noose, drawing the slip rope through the knot, making all thirteen loops disappear as the noose unraveled. "Just having a little fun, Raider."

The big man's face reddened with anger. "I oughta—"

"Later," Earp said. "Doc, leave us be. Go on."

The gambler mockingly tipped his hat. "So long, Raider. Stop by the saloon if you want to pay your respects."

Raider pointed a finger at the red-haired dandy. "The only respects I'm gonna pay will be at your funeral, Holliday."

But the door slammed and the gambler was gone.

Earp sighed, holstering the Buntline. "That man does have a way of gettin' on your nerves."

Raider glanced back at the lawman. "No gun, Marshal?"

Earp shook his head. "No gun. Have a seat, Mr. Raider."

"Just Raider."

Earp gestured toward one of the wooden chairs. "All right. Raider."

But the big man did not immediately sit down. "I don't get it, Earp. Am I free t' go?"

The marshal was about to answer when somebody pushed through the office door. A small, homely woman came in carrying a tray. Earp nodded to her after she had set the tray on his desk. Then the woman hurried out.

Earp pulled back the cloth that covered the tray. "Thought you might be hungry, Raider."

The big man frowned. "I figgered that breakfast was my last meal. Did you bring this for my final dinner?"

"It ain't no such thing, sir. And you don't have to eat it if you don't want to. I just wanted to be more obligin', seein' how I had to lock you up."

"And you ain't gonna hang me?"

"Not yet," Earp replied.

"I'm free t' go?"

The marshal nodded. "Free as a bird. I just wish you'd stay and let me talk to you for a while. Listen to what I have to say."

Raider chortled cynically. "Okay, if I'm free, how about givin' me back my gun?"

Without any hesitation, Earp reached into a desk drawer and took out Raider's holster and gun. He handed them to the big man who immediately strapped on the gun belt. Then he checked the Colt to make sure it was loaded. All six chambers were empty, so Raider filled them with cartridges.

"Are you happy now?" Earp asked.

Raider spun the cylinder of the Colt. "Yeah. I'm real happy."

Earp nodded, his face slacking into an expression of dismay. "Like I said, you're free to go. But I wish you'd stay to hear me out. It won't take long for me to say what's on my mind."

The only thing Raider wanted to do was to find Doc Holliday and whip his ass for the torment he had suffered at the gambler's hands. But something in the marshal's tone made him curious again. And Earp had to be sincere; after all, he had given Raider his gun belt.

The big man pulled a chair closer to Earp's desk. "Okay, Marshal. I reckon I can hear you out. But I want you t' promise me that I'll still be free t' leave when you finish."

Earp nodded. "You have my word."

Raider looked at the tray of food. "Is that ham steak an' potatoes?"

Earp pushed the tray toward him, urging him to eat. Raider shoveled in the food as Earp waited for him to finish. The marshal seemed to have something on his chest. And as soon as Raider's dinner was gone, Earp began to relieve himself of his burden.

When Raider put down his fork, Earp shifted uncomfortably in his chair. "First off," the marshal started, "let me say that I'm almost sure that you didn't kill that man we found in the alley."

Raider leaned back, nodding. "I told you that but you wouldn't listen t' me, Earp."

The marshal bristled a little at Raider's cockiness. "I said almost. If you're as good a Pinkerton as you claim to be, then you should know that no suspect is beyond reproach. Sometimes things can appear one way and be totally different on the other end."

Raider could not disagree with a statement he knew to be the truth.

Earp seemed to take his silence as an affirmation of the statement. He unfolded a piece of paper that he looked at but did not offer to the big man. Instead, he turned his glassy eyes toward the window.

"Sometimes I wonder why I left Kansas City," he said with a hint of sadness in his voice. "But then I see how lawless this territory is and—well, that's no concern of yours."

Raider fought the urge to prod the marshal along. He knew that some men took their time getting to the point. So he listened patiently, as he did not want to incur anymore lawman trouble while he was in Tombstone. He figured to leave as soon as Earp said his piece.

"I took the liberty of wiring your home office," Earp went

on. "They vouched for you and said that you would be valuable in any investigation."

Raider smiled. "They really said that?"

Earp nodded. "A man name of Wagner sent the telegram. I just got it a few minutes ago. That's why I let you out."

"An' I'm obliged, Marshal. Hell, if you believed me from the git-go, we wouldn't have had any trouble at all."

"Don't sit around waitin' for me to apologize," Earp replied coldly. "If you had been in my boots, you would've done the same thing."

Raider wasn't sure about that, but he decided not to buck the lawman. Just hear him out and skeedaddle. No sense putting a burr under anybody's saddle, not since he had been freed.

"The thing is," Earp continued, "you pointed out a lot of stuff that I might never have seen. After I studied on it, I saw it the way you said it. It happened just like you figured. It put me off a little when we were there in the alley. I never saw a lawman who could explain things so clearly from a few clues."

Raider shifted in his chair. "First off, I ain't no lawman. An' second, I was there t' see some o' what had happened. I never said I wasn't in that alley. I just said I didn't kill that poor bastard."

"Bastards," Earp replied.

Raider's brow rose. "Come again?"

Earp folded his hands in front of him. "That one we found wasn't the first dead man that's turned up lately."

The big man leaned forward a little. "I knew it!"

Earp eyed him skeptically. "How'd you know?"

"When we was in the alley," Raider replied. "You said that the dead man was just like the others. That you figgered it had stopped after Blackfist was killed."

Earp sighed. "I got to give it to you, Raider. You know your business. You listen, take note. You ever think about becomin' a marshal?"

"Once, but I was able t' lay down an' rest till the urge passed."

The marshal bristled again at Raider's offhanded manner.

Raider didn't really care if Wyatt Earp was upset or not. "Where'd you find the other two?"

"Didn't find them," the marshal said. "They were brought to me. One from over at Ramsey Canyon, the other from Sierra Vista."

"You got a map?"

Earp nodded, pointing to a frame on the wall behind him. "It's not complete, but I can show you where both places lay."

"So, show me."

The marshal, who was realizing that he had to live with Raider's directness, got up to point out two locations west-southwest of Tombstone. "Mining country," he offered. "Lot of silver over that way."

Raider shifted, trying to shake off the tension in his shoulders.

"Something' wrong?" Earp asked.

"Naw, I just ain't much on silver. Gold neither. Both of 'em can do strange things to a man."

Earp exhaled as he sat down. "You don't have to be a lawman to see that."

"Like I said, I ain't no lawman. You said you thought Blackfist was b'hind the killin's before the third one happened. Why'd you figger it like that?"

"I knew Blackfist was operatin' in these parts. It made sense to me then. At least until I found you in that alley."

"Blackfist ever have a reputation for torturin' his victims?"

Earp shrugged. "He was rough. Said to have beat up a lot of women."

"Beatin' up women don't make you rough," the big man replied. "Any coward can slap around somebody weaker'n him."

"Well, to be honest, until those other two bodies turned up, Blackfist was mainly known for robbin' and for gunfightin'. He faced a few men straight, but he shot some that was un-armed and some in the back. But I never knew him to do— well, you saw it."

"Some spook show, huh?"

Earp lowered his sad eyes. "Just like the others."

"How'd they look? The others, I mean."

Earp shuddered. "Bloody. One of them had been buried. Two prospectors found coyotes digging at it. When they saw what it was, they dug it up and brought it in to me. They seemed to be hoping for a reward, but as far as I could see the man didn't look like any criminal I've known. Hell, didn't even look like much of nothin' human."

Raider eyed the lawman. "Now think on it, Earp. What d' you remember 'bout the body?"

After a few minutes, Earp replied, "He had a rut on his neck." He drew a hand all the way across his throat.

"Deep?" Raider asked. "Like a knife cut?"

"No. It was wide. And—"

"Go on."

Earp straightened his body. "I didn't think of it at the time, but it had a scab on it."

"Which means it could've happened afore he died," Raider replied. "Could've been some kinda torture, same as the one in the alley. Anythin' else?"

"Not on the one that was found at Ramsey Canyon. But the Sierra Vista body was fresh. Two cowhands found it next to a half-dug grave. I reckon they surprised the man who was digging it."

"Did they see him?"

"No, they scared him off beforehand." Earp shook his head. "I never seen a body torn up like that one. Only thing is—well, I ain't even sure I can say it, bein' a Christian man and all—"

"Don't be modest," Raider said. "You ain't gonna hurt my ears. I ain't exactly what you'd call innocent."

"A small cactus," Earp said. "Dry and hard. It was"— Earp blushed but he managed to get it out—"it was shoved up the man's ass! The poor bastard."

"What else?"

Earp gazed disbelievingly at the big man. "That's all you have to say? What else?"

"I'll get sick 'bout it when I find out what it meant," Raider replied. "What else d' you r'member?"

"Not much. Just that somebody had been workin' on them."

Raider leaned back, snorting. "That's puttin' it in a slow runnin' creek. Damn. Did you run out t' either o' those places an' have a look?"

Earp shrugged. "It's not my jurisdiction. I asked around town, to see if anybody had turned up missing. But everybody worth anything was accounted for. I thought it might be Blackfist. Or maybe Indians."

Raider grimaced. "Mebbe. The Apaches and Comanches can tear you a new bunghole when they want to. I never heard of anythin' like that with the Navajo, but Injuns can s'prise you sometimes. Did you check with the local Indian agent?"

Earp nodded. "But he didn't have much to say. Claims there hasn't been any trouble for a while."

"I ain't heard of any."

"Nor had I."

They were quiet for a few minutes.

Raider finally stood up. "Well, Marshal, I reckon I'll be on my way now."

Earp frowned at him. "You're leavin'?"

A shrug of the tall Pinkerton's wide shoulders. "You said I was free t' go. I am, ain't I?"

"Raider, sit down."

Raider's hand fell next to the redwood handle of the Colt. "Ain't partial t' bein' told what t' do, Earp."

The lawman had to put the lid on his rising temper. "All right. Please sit down. I'm asking."

"Look here, Earp. I got work t' do. My agency is gonna be wantin' t' send me on another case. An' they prob'ly ain't too happy 'bout you puttin' me in lockup. Hell, they'll blame me for any trouble I get in. An' far as I can see, Tombstone is a place where trouble ain't hard t' find."

Earp unfolded a piece of paper and handed it to Raider. "This came today."

Raider eyed the crudely scrawled telegraph message. It was from Wagner, telling him to render any assistance to Wyatt Earp and to advise if there was a case at hand. He was to assess the situation and reply if the territory of Arizona or the town of Tombstone wanted to pay for his services.

"Damn," he muttered. "Things must be slow at the home office."

"I beg your pardon?"

Raider plopped back down in the chair. "Nothin'. Just go ahead an' say what's on your mind."

Earp stiffened indignantly, but he went on in a prideful manner. "As much as it grieves me to do so, I have to admit that this thing is beyond my powers as a lawman. My territory extends only so far. And it does not extend to the mining areas. I've always left them alone. I have enough trouble here without worrying about a bunch of heathen miners. It's bad enough when they come to town once a month."

"Let me see if I can save you some breath," Raider offered. "You want me t' stay here an' look into this. See if I can figger out who killed those three men an' why they killed 'em."

"That's accurate."

Raider stood up again. "I'll think on it."

"I need your answer now."

He pointed a finger at the lawman. "Now look here, Earp, I can't be buffaloed. If I tell you I'll think on it, I will. An' when I give you my answer, it'll be in my own good time."

"I won't stand for your attitude!"

Raider shrugged. "Then forget 'bout hirin' me. It all comes in the same saddlebag, Marshal. I ain't stayed alive this long 'cause I let every greenhorn tell me what t' do."

Earp scowled at him.

"Not t' say you're a greenhorn, Marshal. You got a tough job an' you're just doin' it the best you know how. Same as me. But you locked me up an' I took it, so now you can take a little waitin'. I promise you'll have my answer afore sundown."

Earp started to say something but Raider extended his hand, stopping him. "Shake on it, Marshal."

Earp seemed to back off. "By sundown?"

Raider nodded.

They shook on it.

Raider wanted to make some joke about washing his hand, but he figured it wouldn't be right.

"I'll talk t' you later, Marshal."

"That's all well and good," Earp replied, "but I still have to warn you to step lively in my town. I don't care if you are a Pinkerton, you still obey the law."

"I plan to, Marshal. I sure as hell wouldn't wanna end up on Boot Hill. Not t'day, anyhow. Course, if we was t' draw on each other, who's t' say which of us they'd plant?"

He turned away from Earp's disapproving glare, exiting without looking back at the lawman.

A grin spread over his face when he hit the street. It felt good to be free again. First he wanted to check his belongings at the stable and then he wanted to find Doc Holliday and get even with him. No need to tell Earp that he had already decided to take the case. Not until sundown, anyway.

CHAPTER TWELVE

The sun baked the small town of Tombstone, making it sweat like an old stick of dynamite. As he strode toward the stable, Raider felt as if he had landed on a powder keg that was ready to blow. Wyatt Earp, who was probably the toughest marshal he had ever encountered, was noticably shaken by the three bizarre deaths that had occured in and around his town. Still, for all Earp's hard-as-nails backbone, the lawman did not have the keen eye for detail that a Pinkerton used on every case. Earp knew where the forest was, but he definitely had trouble finding his way between the trees.

Three men dead, Raider thought. And all of them tortured. His heart started to pound. The questions came into his head. *Who? Why? Where?*

Earp had mentioned two places. Sierra Vista and Ramsey Canyon. The bodies had been found at those locations. Best to start where the trail was warm. Of course, he'd also have another look in the alley behind the stable. Maybe something would turn up there. The first time he searched, it had been dark and Earp had been there with his guns and his deputies.

Raider touched the handle of his Colt. It felt good to be

armed again. The gun made things a whole lot easier.

When he reached the stable, he found the smith lying back on a pile of hay sipping from a brown jug. He sat up when Raider walked in. His face and body were soaked with sweat from the heat.

"Came back to check on my stuff," Raider said.

The smith nodded. "It's all up there, safe and sound."

Raider climbed the ladder to the loft. True to smithy's word, the big man's gear had not been touched. Raider hesitated, wondering if he should saddle up right away and head west to scout the locations where the bodies had been found. He decided to wait and get a frest start the next morning. Until then he could poke around Tombstone and see what else floated to the top of the rain barrel.

As he descended, the smithy stood up. "See, I told you. You can trust me, sir. I mean, even when they locked you in the jail, I said to myself, 'That man's honest as the day is long. He'll be back to get his stuff.' And it turns out that I was right."

Raider thanked him.

The smith held out the jug. "You want a snort?"

Raider thought it over and came to the conclusion that one wouldn't hurt. He took a long pull from the crock, tasting the worst corn whiskey that he had ever had in his life. It burned a hole all the way to his gut.

"Made it myself," the smith said.

Raider coughed, rubbing his mouth with the back of his hand. "Next time lay off the coal oil."

The smith laughed. "Tasted it, did you? It always gives it a little more kick."

Raider handed the jug back to him. "I'd like to say I've tasted worse but that'd be a lie."

"Aw, I don't take no offense. Hey, are you really a Pinkerton? I mean, that's been all the talk in town."

Raider grimaced. Now everybody in the whole damned territory probably knew a Pinkerton was in the area. So much for disguises and false identities.

"You got a name, smithy?"

"Walter. Walter Mason."

Raider looked him squarely in the face. "All right, Walter. You know who I am. But you don't know why I'm here."

Walter shook his head. "No, that I don't know."

Raider wondered how much he should tell the man. "There's trouble hereabouts, Walter. Lots o' trouble."

"What kind of trouble?"

Raider shrugged. "Big trouble. You'll hear 'bout it soon enough. Right now I was wonderin' if you could help me."

Walter looked dumbfounded. "Help you?"

"You know anythin' 'bout the mines west o' here?"

Walter rubbed his chin. "Well, I've done some work for the miners. And once in a while the mining companies have me shoe their draft horses. But I don't really—"

"Which mines did you work for?"

"Well, the Sierra Silver Company for one. And what was that other one?"

Raider tipped back his Stetson. "Take your time. Just see if you can remember the name."

"Ransom Ore Mines," Walter said finally. "Yeah. Ransom Ore."

Raider nodded appreciatively. "You wouldn't happen t' know the top kick in those outfits?"

"No," Walter replied, "just the name. I never met the bosses, just the hired man who brought the horses to me."

"Never went out to the mines yourself?"

"No."

Raider exhaled. "Ransom Ore and Sierra Silver. Where are they?"

Walter scratched his head. "Well, Ransom is over by Ramsey Canyon and—"

"Sierra Vista is the other one."

Walter frowned. "Yeah. How'd you know?"

"Just a lucky guess. Damn."

Bodies found at two different locations, near two different mines, almost like they had been planted. Best not to jump to conclusions though, at least until he had taken a look. His head was racing with the urge to know. The old intuition had kicked in. It always felt like that when he was on a case.

"I want my horse ready t' go t'morrow afore sunup," he told the smith. "That square with you?"

"No problem," Walter replied. "I'm usually up before daybreak. It's too hot to work during the day anymore. Summer is always like this."

Raider figured he was due for a cool bath, but he had to take care of other business first.

He flipped the smithy a silver dollar and left the stable. He wanted to send a wire to Chicago, to make sure that Wagner really knew he was working for Wyatt Earp. No sense taking any chances that the marshal might have cooked up a scheme to have Raider work for free. He had to consider the possibility that, despite what he said, Earp still thought Raider was a suspect in the killings. Maybe he had let the big man go so he could keep an eye on him, maybe follow him to the truth. A reply from Wagner could settle all doubts.

As he passed the bathhouse, he saw the Chinese woman standing in the window, staring out at the street. Raider paused to tip his hat to her. She smiled wryly and moved away from the window. Yes, he'd surely have a bath when he was finished working.

After the telegram had been sent to the home office, Raider returned to the alley where the dead man had been found. Hunkering in front of the hay shed, he tried to remember what he had seen and heard. The killer had been talking to his victim. Something about retribution. That was the only word Raider could actually remember.

So then what?

The murderer tortured the victim until Raider shouted out in the darkness. Hearing the intrusion, the killer immediately finished off his prey, putting a gun to the victim's head and squeezing the trigger. Then he ran. Fast, like a young, healthy man. Had he figured that Raider would help the dead man before he went after the killer?

Raider followed the escape route down the alley. He stopped to look at the bullet holes that had been made by slugs meant for him. The killer had been aiming for his head. Maybe he was a good shot. Or a bad shot. After all, he had missed.

Shaking off a chill that comes with cheating death, the big man strode on to the place where the blood had been found the night before. It was still there, though it had baked dry in the heat. Raider hunkered down, like a killer who was hiding from his pursuer. From the position of the blood, it appeared that the man had been wounded in the right hand. Which meant he was carrying his pistol in his left hand. No way to tell which was his natural gun hand.

Raider had probably wounded him with his first shot. Then he made it to the end of the alley. The distance didn't seem as great in the light. Had the murderer been discovered during the day, Raider would have hit him squarely with his Colt. At night, it was a completely different shot.

At the end of the alley he examined the hoofprints again. An ordinary lawman, even Wyatt Earp, wouldn't have noticed the slight discoloration in the tracks. There was a rusty tint to the inside of the hoofprint. The hue contrasted with the darker soil of Tombstone's street dirt. Several small clods of the same rust-colored earth lay at the bottom of the track. Red dirt terrain. Something to think about when he got started.

As he turned to retrace his steps, a brassy glint caught his eye. He hadn't seen it before, but the sun was now behind him and the rays had reflected off something wedged in the stays of a rain barrel. The reflection was in the same place where the killer had been kneeling.

Raider used the knife from his boot to dig the object out of the rain barrel. Nothing but a brass button. It was small, round, and bore the initials of the U.S. Army. From the few threads still clinging to the shank it appeared to have come from the sleeve of a blue officer's coat. Raider slipped the button into his pocket, searching for a while before he decided to give it up.

Only a few hours of sunlight were left and he wanted to get cleaned up before he spoke to Earp. He'd share what little he had learned with the marshal and ask him some more questions in the bargain. His nose was to the ground now and he wouldn't stop until he reached the end of the trail.

The Chinese woman turned around when he entered the bathhouse. He looked at her through the steam that rose off the tub. Her black hair was limp and dull, a moist gleam on her tawny skin. Her thick lips parted slightly,

"Am I too early?" Raider asked.

The girl's face slacked into a frown. "My father is not here."

He shrugged. "So I cain't have a bath?"

She lifted her chin. "Lock the front door."

Raider obliged her.

She helped him get undressed. Her eyes bulged when she saw the massive thickness of his member. Raider figured he was going to have one last moment of fun before he jumped into his case with both feet.

"I want a cold tub," he told her.

She led him back to a wooden tub in the rear of the building. "There."

Raider eased down into the soothing liquid. He leaned back and closed his eyes. The woman disappeared for a moment. Probably going to take off her clothes, the big man thought, so she could join him in the tub.

But it never happened that way. After a few minutes of soaking, he heard the voices rise up in an argument. It took him a while to figure out that the girl's father had come back and was now chiding her for letting a man bathe while he was not there.

Raider sighed. There wasn't going to be any excitement after all—until he ran into Doc Holliday again.

He was clean and shaved when he started for Earp's office. He took the route past the saloon, where he happened to look in and see Doc Holliday dealing faro. Raider stopped dead still, looking at the man who had tormented him in Earp's jail cell. Of course, the good doctor had only been having a little fun, something that Raider intended to do now.

Since Holliday hadn't seen him, Raider managed to lean against the wall of the saloon's facade, keeping out of the gambler's sight. How was he going to repay Doc? It had to be good, something that scared the living shit out of him.

Then it hit him; the place where Holliday would be most vulnerable. It was almost a childish trick, something that Raider never did. But Holliday had it coming and it seemed like the best way to pay him back.

Doc Holliday rose from the gaming table. "Gentlemen, if you will excuse me, I shall return shortly."

One of the card players frowned at him. "Where you think you're goin', Doc? I won that last hand an' I'm ready to win another one."

"Don't worry," Holliday replied. "You'll get a chance to

lose what you've won. But I have to see a man about a horse."

They all laughed because they knew that he meant he was going to relieve himself in the outhouse.

Holliday exited through a side door, stepping down an alley that was rich with the shadows of late afternoon and early evening. He smiled a little. He had managed to lose a few hands to satisfy the tinhorns and he was still way ahead on the day. Not a bad way to make a living.

He reached for the handle of the outhouse door.

No, not a bad way to—

Holliday felt a hand on the back of his neck. He reached for his knife but another hand caught his wrist. Somebody pushed him facedown into the hole of the outhouse seat.

"You son of a bitch!" Holliday cried.

He struggled but his assailant had a superior weight advantage.

The smell of lye and feces gagged the gambler.

"So, they're puttin' up a gallows," Raider said, holding Holliday down. "And you were gonna tie the rope."

Holliday tried to yell at the big Pinkerton but he couldn't find his breath in the stench of the shithouse.

"Say you give," Raider offered, "an' I'll let you up."

Holliday started to cough uncontrollably.

Raider suddenly felt sorry for the man. So he made a big mistake. He let Holliday come up for air.

The gambler swung hard with his right hand, catching Raider in the gut. The big man grunted, but he managed to shove Holliday backward. When Holliday bounced off the stall and came back toward him, Raider had his gun drawn and butted against the temple of the gambler's head.

"No more bullshit," Raider said.

Holliday was grinning. "Look down, Pinkerton."

Raider didn't have to look. Holliday pressed the point of the knife blade against his cotton shirt. They froze there, locked in a standoff.

"We're both pretty fast," Holliday offered.

Raider kept the Colt on his temple. "Too fast. Why didn't you go ahead an' stick me?"

Holliday shrugged. "You could've shot me."

"I'll ease off if you will."

The gambler hesitated. "That was a mean trick to play on me."

"Any meaner'n you standin' there with that goddamn rope, sayin' they was gonna string me up?"

Holliday started to laugh. "That was a good one, wasn't it?"

Raider had to grin. "Aw, you bastard!"

"You were shitting your pants, Pinkerton. And if you don't let me use the outhouse, I'm going to shit mine!"

They were still laughing when Holliday closed the door to the outhouse.

"That's a pretty good one, Pinkerton!"

"Yeah, I just thought it up a few minutes ago. I knew you'd go to the john sooner or later. You didn't make me wait long."

Holliday came out after a while. "You want to play cards? I got a table full of—"

He started coughing again.

Raider frowned, wishing he could do something for the gambler.

"Come on," Holliday said. "I want to introduce you to somebody."

"I got bus'ness," Raider replied.

Holliday looked sideways at him. "Yeah? So Wyatt asked you to help, huh? Did you tell him yes?"

"No, but I will afore sundown. Which ain't that far away. Say, Holliday, what you know 'bout all this?"

The gambler shrugged. "Just that somebody has killed three people and he hasn't been too delicate about how he killed them."

"He? You got any ideas who it might be?"

"No. Not really."

"Then it could be a woman," Raider offered.

Holliday smiled. "I never thought of that. So, what, if anything, have you learned?"

"Two of those bodies were found up near the mines," Raider replied. "The Sierra and Ransom mines. Know anythin' 'bout 'em?"

"They come to town and I take their money. I've never even seen a silver mine. Although I have dragged my share of ore across the table. I—"

The cough returned. Holliday wiped his mouth with a

handkerchief. "Come on, Pinkerton. I'll introduce you to somebody who's worked up at the mines. He might know something."

"A miner?"

"No, a—"

But he coughed until they reached the stairs with the sign at the bottom. It read: "Granville Bascomb, Medical Doctor. Take the steps." An arrow pointed upward.

Raider helped Holliday up the stairs. The gambler seemed to have been weakened by their ruckus. The big man was sorry that he had played the joke on Holliday. He hadn't taken the gambler's condition into consideration.

When they knocked on the door, a kindly old gentleman greeted them and ushered them into his office. It smelled like tinctures and potions. Bascomb was a real doctor, Raider thought. He even had plaques and sheepskins on the walls, credentials from colleges back east.

Bascomb smiled warmly when he saw Holliday. His countenance sported bushy, gray eyebrows that moved as his face shifted its expression. Weak blue eyes, gray head, thin, pale lips. He was an old-timer, though Raider thought he was sprier than he looked. He helped Holliday into a wooden chair.

"Is your consumption bothering you?" Bascomb asked.

Holliday nodded. "I was hoping you could help me again."

Bascomb went to a cabinet and came back carrying a small, brown bottle. "Here," he told the gambler. "Just like the last time. I don't know how much it will help, but if it makes you fell better—"

Holliday took a small swig from the bottle. Almost immediately, he began to breathe a little easier. Raider watched as he filled his lungs, gulping for air. It wasn't a pretty sight, a grown man drowning in his own juices.

Bascomb turned his impish face toward Raider. "My good man, were you in need of some medical attention?"

"Er, no, not just now. I'm with Holliday here. He started coughin' so I came with him. He seems to be doin' better since you gave him that medicine."

Bascomb shrugged. "It's an opium tincture. And you'd better be careful, Doctor Holliday. You know what happened the last time I gave you a bottle of that tincture. You almost went to sleep permanently!"

Raider frowned at the gambler. "What happened?"

Holliday had recovered enough to talk. "I took too much of this good stuff and stiffened up like a board. The girls at the hacienda thought I was a goner for sure. Hell, I just slept it off."

Bascomb shook a fatherly finger at Holliday. "You shouldn't make light of that. Life is a precious thing."

"Like I told you before, Doctor Bascomb, I'm—"

"I know, I know," Bascomb said. "You're dying from the inside out. But I'd think you'd want to enjoy what valuable time you have left."

"I got plenty of time," Holliday replied.

"Listen to the man," Raider urged. "Only a fool would try t' kill hisself afore it was his time t' go."

Bascomb turned and nodded at Raider. "You're a wise man, sir. If ever you need my attention, I would be willing to give you a lower rate."

Raider twirled his Stetson in his hands. "Well, sir, there is somethin' that you might be able t' give me. Holliday here said that you've worked up at the mines some. I'd like t' ask a few questions if it's not too much trouble."

Bascomb shrugged. "I have had some experience treating the miners. You know, the usual injuries. Stitching up a cut forehead or wrapping a smashed finger. Once in a while somebody loses a limb, but there's not much I can do about that. I've had to saw off my share of legs, I can tell you that."

"How long you been workin' in these parts?"

Bascomb cleared his throat. "I've only come west in the past three years," the doctor replied. "I admit that I waited rather late in life to seek my fortune in the territories. But so far it hasn't been bad to me at all. Even this past year in Tombstone has been profitable."

"No shortage of sick and hurt men in this place," Holliday offered. "Even if most of them can't pay you."

Bascomb glared at the gambler. "I don't suppose you have what you owe me, Doctor Holliday?"

Holliday reached into his pocket and took out a twenty dollar gold piece. "Here's a double eagle, Doctor Bascomb.

That should take care of what I owe you and give me credit for another bottle of this potion."

Bascomb sighed. "It will probably kill you. Along with the drink and the tobacco. I'd rather see you alive than have you settle your arrears."

"How long you been dealin' with the mines?" Raider asked.

"Less than a year," Bascomb replied. "I don't like to make the ride out there too often. Although I am due to go out to Ramsey Canyon tomorrow."

"To the Ransom Mine?" Raider asked.

Bascomb nodded. "May have to take off another leg."

Holliday smiled appreciatively at the tall Pinkerton. "You didn't waste any time gathering your facts, Raider."

Raider waved him off. "Just two names. Ransom and Sierra. You ever deal with either of 'em, Doctor Bascomb?"

"Yes, I have treated men for both outfits."

Raider shifted on his feet, hitching up his gun belt a little. "What I have to ask now is strictly 'tween us, Doctor."

Bascomb said he was agreeable.

"Just this," Raider started. "Have either one o' those minin' comp'nies complained lately 'bout men disappearin'?"

"Not that I know of," Bascomb said, frowning. "Why? Is there a problem out there? Because I don't want to ride all the way out to Ramsey Canyon if there's going to be trouble."

"I think you'll be all right," Raider said. "Just don't ride back after dark. Hell, you can even ride back with me if I see you there."

Bascomb seemed concerned about something.

"You okay?" Raider asked.

Bascomb nodded, but then said: "I think you should be forewarned. Levon Ransom is not the kind of man to be pushed around."

"Much obliged," the big man replied. "I'll keep that under my hat. You wanna ride out with me t'morrow, Doctor Bascomb? I'll be leavin' just afore sunup."

"I'm not a rooster," Bascomb said. "I'll leave a little later. Besides, I'm driving a buggy and you'll no doubt be on horseback."

Holliday clapped the older man on the back. "Thank you, Doctor. You've been a big help to both of us."

Bascomb glanced at Raider. "Sir, if I can be of any more assistance to you, feel free to ask."

"Much obliged."

All three men shook hands and then Raider followed Holliday toward the stairs. It was getting close to dark. Time to go tell Earp that he had accepted the case. Then he'd get a good night's sleep and start fresh in the morning.

"He's a pretty good ol' boy," Raider offered.

"Doc Bascomb? Yeah, he's a real godsend. Hard to figure how an old timer like him ended up in this place. But he gets the job done."

They hit the street and Raider started to explain how the wanderlust set in on men at all times in their lives. Besides, he argued, how could anybody live back east? It was so crowded, or at least he had heard it said.

Holliday was agreeing with him, explaining his own migration west, when the man came toward them in the street.

"Holliday!"

It was one of the men who had been gambling in the saloon.

"Shit," the gambler said under his breath. "He thinks I walked out on him. I hope I don't have to kill him."

But the man had already pulled a gun and he was raising it to aim at Holliday, who started to cough at the worst time.

Raider drew quickly, firing one shot that knocked the pistol from the angry man's hand. The man danced around, clutching his wrist. Raider went over and picked up the pocket revolver that had fallen into the street.

He pointed toward the doctor's office. "Go on, pilgrim. Doc Bascomb will patch you up."

The man ran toward the stairs without another word of protest.

Holliday watched him go. "Damn, you saved my hide again, Pinkerton. I reckon I owe you."

Raider was going to say something, but he heard another voice echoing in the street. Wyatt Earp strode down the avenue with his shotgun drawn. His two deputies were behind him. Raider was pretty sure the marshal would want an explanation as to why he was shooting again.

CHAPTER THIRTEEN

Wyatt Earp rested the shotgun on his hip, glaring at the two grinning troublemakers who avoided his steely gaze. "I mighta known I'd find one of you close to where the shootin' started. And here I find both of you."

Raider turned to face the marshal. "Aw, that tinhorn there was tryin' t' kill Doc, so I just winged him a little. Sent him on to the sawbones so he could get his hand patched up. No trouble, Wyatt."

Holliday echoed the big man. "Yeah, no trouble, Wyatt. We even spared the town the cost of another plantin' on Boot Hill. So don't go getting your back up."

One of the deputies gestured with the barrel of a Winchester. "Want me to take 'em in, Marshal?"

Earp sighed, casting a glance toward Doc Bascomb's office. "You say the man went up there for treatment?"

Raider nodded. "He probably won't die. I had the angle on him. Hell, I was just tryin' to keep him from pluggin' Doc."

"Yeah," the gambler said, "he was just trying to keep that tinhorn from plugging me."

Earp gave his ne'er-do-well friend a sidelong glance. "If

you ask me, plugging both of you wouldn't be a bad idea right now."

"You need my help," Raider offered. "Don't you, Marshal Earp?"

One of the deputies frowned at the big man. "What's he mean by that, Marshal? You gonna hire him as a deputy?"

Earp waved his men away. "Go on your rounds."

Both of them hesitated, no doubt wondering if the Pinkerton planned to take their jobs away from them.

"Hurry it along," Earp commanded. "And make sure the back door is locked at the general store."

"Yes, sir."

"Right away, Marshal."

When they were out of earshot, Earp tipped back his Stetson. "I need your answer now, Raider. Are you going to assist me in this investigation? Or will you ride out? Either way, I need to know."

"It ain't quite sundown yet," the big man replied, pointing to the sky.

Earp seemed to inflate again. "Confound it, man, you gave me your word."

"Afore nightfall—that's what I said. And I aim to keep my promise. But I have t' make one more stop afore I tell you. Come on, it's on the way to your office."

Earp turned away from them and stomped angrily down the dusty street.

Holliday whistled through his teeth. "Damn it all, Raider, I've never seen anybody get Wyatt's goat the way you do!"

Raider chuckled. "He does wear his suspenders a little tight. But hell, he's a good lawman. I can see that."

Holliday frowned a little. "Yeah, maybe too good."

"What's that supposed to mean?"

A deep sigh from the gambler. "One day he's not going to tolerate men like you and me. Then he's got two choices. Run us out of town or kill us."

Raider clapped his new-found friend on the shoulder. "Let's hope it never comes t' that. Come on, Doc. I want you there when I talk t' him."

"Me?"

"I might need your help later."

Holliday shook his head. "Look, Raider, I know I owe you

for shooting the gun out of that tinhorn's hand, but in case you haven't noticed, I'm not exactly what you would call a do-gooder. My place is in the saloon, dealing poker and taking money from card-playing fools."

Raider figured the man had a point. "Well, Doc, if that's the way you feel 'bout it, I never been one t' ask a man t' go agin his beliefs."

"You come out to the hacienda some time and I'll buy you a drink," the gambler offered. "Maybe even treat you to some of that Mexican delight."

Raider extended his hand. "Shake on it?"

Doc Holliday shook his hand. "And one more thing, Raider."

"What's that?"

"If you ever try to stick my head in the outhouse shithole again, I'm going to run my knife right through your gut."

Raider smiled a little. "Well, Holliday, I'll keep that in mind the next time you start tyin' a hangman's knot for me."

"Fair enough. I better get back to the saloon before some-body else decides to shoot me."

They fell into stride, heading along the main thoroughfare.

Holliday broke away and went into the saloon, leaving Raider to head for the telegraph office. He wanted to see if Wagner had replied to his inquiry earlier in the day. Would the wire office be open this late?

As he stepped up onto the porch of the building, he heard the telegraph key clicking away. The key operator sat in the shadows, taking down the message.

"Say, is there a—"

The operator waved him off impatiently. "I'm tryin' to lis-ten here."

Raider felt justly chastized. "Sorry."

The key rattled for a few more minutes and then stopped.

Raider gazed over the counter at the key man. "I was in here earlier and I sent a—"

"If you don't mind," the man replied indignantly, "I still haven't finished with this wire."

"But the key—"

"I just wrote down the code, sir. Now I have to string it all together and decipher the message."

Raider figured the man was acting a little huffy, but he let it go. No sense starting trouble, even if the man could have used a lesson in manners. He leaned against the counter, waiting as patiently as he could. Outside the shadows were growing longer, cooling the hot day. Raider would have to hurry if he was to keep his word to Earp and give him an answer by nightfall.

The key man struck a match to torch the wick of a storm lamp. When the circle of red light swelled in the office, the man gaped at Raider and then at the message he had been working on. He went to work with his pencil, feverishly deciphering the code.

Raider watched until the man looked up.

"Sorry," he said, rubbing his eyes. "I haven't been at this too long. I used to work for the railroad."

"Sometimes a man needs a change in his work," Raider offered. "Do you remember me? I was in here today. Sent a wire all the way back to Chicago. I was wonderin' if the reply came."

The man looked at the piece of paper he had been working on. "Is your name Raider?"

"That'd be me."

"This last message just come in for you. I was ready to lock the doors when the key started. Want me to read it to you, or do you want a copy?"

Raider shrugged. "I trust you. But make it quick."

The man cleared his throat. "Says, 'You are to co—co—"

"Cooperate?"

"Yeah, that's it. How'd you know?"

"Keep readin'."

"Says to—what you said. And to 'the full extent of Marshal Earp's needs, at the regular daily fee.' That's it. And it come from a man name of William Wagner."

Raider tipped his hat. "Much obliged, sir."

He tossed a nickle on the counter, for the man's trouble.

As he strode back out into the street, he gazed over his shoulder to see the last sliver of sun as it fell to the west.

"Right on time."

He kept on, heading for the marshal's office.

The Chinese woman waved to him as he passed the bathhouse. Her father quickly appeared to whisk her away, then returned to shoot a dirty look at the big man from Arkansas.

Raider smiled and politely tipped his hat, thinking that the girl might be a whole lot of fun without her father around to guard her. Best to leave it alone though. No need to cause any more trouble.

Earp was behind his desk when Raider pushed into the office. "Well?" he challenged with an expectant expression on his doleful face. "It's sundown."

Raider nodded. "I'm your man, Marshal. But it's gonna cost the citizens of Tombstone."

"What's the going rate?"

"Settle that with the home office," the big man replied. "We can talk in the meantime."

"I'll send for some supper," Earp offered. "You take coffee?"

Raider shook his head. "No. Whiskey."

Earp bristled, but he did not protest. He wasn't too happy about the big man's drinking, but the marshal did seem glad to have Raider on the job.

Earp watched warily as Raider poured himself the second after-dinner shot of whiskey. It was the good stuff from the saloon. Smooth Irish whiskey, Raider's favorite. As he knocked back the hooch, he had to wonder if Earp and the citizens of Tombstone were picking up the tab for the meal.

"Where do you aim to start?" Earp asked.

Raider slammed the shotglass on the marshal's desk and reached for the bottle. "I already started." He threw down a third swallow.

Earp shifted in his chair. "I beg your pardon."

"I knew when I left here that I'd prob'ly take the case," Raider replied. "So I went back t' the alley where we found that man."

"Find anything?"

Raider dug into his pocket and pulled out the brass button he had found on the rain barrel in the alley. "Take a look at this." He tossed it on the desk in front of the marshal.

Earp closely examined the button, holding it in the light of an oil lamp. "Brass," he said. "Marked with *U.S.*, which means it probably came off the coat of a soldier."

"I figger from the sleeve of an officer's coat," Raider offered. "Mebbe Cavalry."

Earp gave him back the button. "Oh, it's off the coat of an officer all right. But not a cavalry officer and probably not off the coat of any western army soldier."

Raider studied the brass markings, running his finger over the letters. "How you figger that?"

Earp shrugged. "Simple. Cavalry officers don't have buttons on the sleeves of their coats. A button might get caught in the reins. They wear gloves, too. But I can't ever remember seein' any kind of soldier with this sort of button on his sleeve. Leastways, not west of the Mississippi."

Raider put the button back into his coat pocket. "Well, I'll keep that in mind." He wasn't sure if Earp was right or not. The marshal might have been trying to show off.

"If you don't believe me," the marshal rejoined, "check over at Fort Huachuca. Or Fort Bowie."

Raider lifted his hands in defeat. "Hey, I ain't takin' it personal, Wyatt. I'm willin' t' listen t' whatever you got t' say."

The marshal rubbed his hands together. "I'm more interested in what you got to say, Pinkerton. Did you find anything else in that alley?"

"Dirt," Raider replied.

Earp's brow fretted. "Come again?"

"In the hoofprints from the horse that ran away with our killer."

The marshal looked skeptical. "What has that got to do with anything? There's dirt all over this territory."

"Yeah, but the dirt in that alley is darker than the red dirt I found in those hoofprints, which means that the killer was ridin' somewhere in the red stuff. It may not be much, but I might be able to use it later on down the trail."

Earp leaned forward a little. "Are you sayin' that you got down and looked inside the hoofprint of a horse? And you found that the dirt in the print was a different color?"

"A horse's hooves will carry clods of wet dirt for miles," the big man offered. "That's all I'm sayin'."

The marshal shook his head. "I've had a pain in my noggin ever since you showed up here, Raider."

"Well, if that's all, I'd like to get some sleep—"

He started to stand up.

Earp waved him back into his seat. "We're not finished

yet, sir. I have a few things I want to share with you."

"I need a fresh start t'morrow," Raider went on. "If I—"

"Don't worry," the marshal said, "you'll get plenty of time to gamble and whore with Doc Holliday."

"But that ain't—"

Earp took something out of his desk drawer, holding it on his lap. "You aren't the only one who was busy today. While you were shooting up my town, I paid a visit to the undertaker."

"Undertaker?"

"Remember," Earp replied with a sly smile, "the corpse we found was wearing a pair of pants. You suggested at the time that we look through the pockets of the dead man's trousers."

Raider pointed at the bundle on Earp's lap. "So you've got the pants right there?"

Earp tossed them on his desktop. "Nothing special. The kind of denim pants you'd fine on any cowpoke, miner, drifter, farmer. The general store probably sells several pairs each day."

"So if there's nothin' special 'bout them, why do you—"

"I found this inside them," Earp said, holding up a piece of paper.

Raider asked to see the paper.

Earp said it didn't matter. He knew what it was. A pay marker from the Sierra Silver Company. He started to explain what a pay marker was, but Raider beat him to it.

"I know all 'bout it, Marshal. Our agency was one of the first t' suggest pay markers to the mining companies. Timber comp'nies too."

"All right, Mr. Smart Aleck, what's a pay marker?"

Raider shrugged, smiling. "Well, since there are a lotta payroll robberies, the minin' comp'nies arrange in advance for the bank t' hold their payroll money. When it's payday, those miners who don't want t' take their pay in silver can bring a pay marker t' the bank an' pick up their money. Looks like the man in the alley didn't make it."

"Lucius," Earp said. "His name was Lucius McCabe. It's written right here on the marker."

Raider held out his hand. "Just let me take a look. It won't kill you. Even if it does hurt your pride."

Earp threw him the pay marker. Raider examined it closely,

seeing that it did indeed have the name Lucius McCabe on it. Lucius hadn't gotten his money, otherwise the bank would have retained the marker.

"Did you check at the bank to see if Lucius picked up his pay last month or the month before?"

Earp smiled like a possum. "Yes, I did."

Raider smiled. "Good for you."

"Lucius McCabe picked up his pay the month before last, but he never came for his pay last month. So there!"

Raider leaned back, rubbing his chin. "Then that means Lucius McCabe got into trouble sometime after he got his pay marker, but afore he could come into town t' pick up his pay. Which prob'ly means he was kidnapped either on payday or the day after."

It was Earp's turn to scoff. "Now there's no way in the world that you could know that."

Raider eyed the marshal. "Okay, you tell me. How many minin' rats you ever know that let a pay marker stay hot in their pockets? Any man that mines for another man is gonna be broke an' thirsty on payday. The first thing he's gonna do is ride hellbent into town an' get his money. The second thing is get drunk and third thing is a woman—"

"All right!" the lawman bellowed.

"Ain't you forgittin' somethin'?" Raider challenged.

Earp was steaming. "I don't know what you mean."

"When we found that dead man, we also found a hatchet. You remember, the one that the killer was usin' t' work on him."

Earp nodded, easing back a little. "I didn't forget. I got it right here if you want to look at it."

Raider grinned. "You're doin' pretty good at playin' detective, Marshal. S'pose you tell me somethin' 'bout that hatchet."

Earp sighed. "Well, it's not the kind of tool you'd regularly find at a mine. It's not a pick ax, or even a hammer."

"So where would you find it? Regular-like, I mean?"

"Probably by a woodpile," the marshal replied. "It's barely big enough to split kindling."

Raider held out his hands. "Sounds fine t' me."

"You want to see it?"

"I'll pass, Marshal. You just keep it safe in case I want t' see it later."

They were quiet for a couple of seconds.

Earp looked over the desk at the big Pinkerton. "What do you plan to do next?"

Raider leaned forward. "I'm gonna ride out t' the Sierra Silver Company. I understand it's west o' here."

"South-southwest," Earp replied. "Near Sierra Vista."

"In the mountains?"

The marshal nodded. "There's woods up that way too, so watch yourself."

"Wanna ride along?"

"No. Why would I?"

Raider shrugged his shoulders. "Just thought you'd wanna make sure the good citizens of Tombstone get their money's worth."

Earp pointed a finger at him. "Now look here, Raider, I don't care if I have to hire you to help solve this thing. I mean, if it's goin' on out there at the mines, then sooner or later it's bound to turn up here."

"It already has," the big man reminded him.

"Yes, and I'll have no more of it. But this town is not paying for your services. I'm taking the money out of my own pocket. So don't go around telling everyone that the town is paying you. Because it's not. Is that clear?"

Raider nodded. "Your secret is safe."

Earp shook his head. "This whole business is damnable."

"It sure is. So I figger after I go t' the Sierra Silver Company, I might pay a visit to the Ransom Ore Mines."

The lawman frowned. "Be careful around there. Levon Ransom doesn't take kindly to trespassers. He's had more than one man try to jump his claim."

"I'll be careful, Wyatt."

He stood up, turning to the door.

"And one more thing," Earp added. "Call me Marshal!"

Raider gave him a mocking salute. "Yes, sir, Marshal!"

"And check in with me every day!"

"If I get the chance, Wyatt. If I get the chance!"

He went out, slamming the door behind him, stomping into the street.

"Lawmen," he said under his breath.

He started for the stable. As he passed the saloon, he could almost hear the money hitting the green felt of Doc Holliday's gaming table. Then he went by the bathhouse only to see the Chinese woman staring out at him again. He had to fight off both urges. Probably he shouldn't even have had the three shots of whiskey at supper. He wanted his head to be clear the next day. He had to find out who killed Lucius McCabe and the other two unfortunate souls.

Best just to go back to the stable and sleep until daybreak. Put everything else out of his mind. He'd have some fun as soon as the case was solved.

Raider lay back on his saddle, staring at the dark ceiling of the stable loft. It was a moonless night, with a cool breeze stirring the air to dissipate the heat of the day. Tombstone was quiet.

So why couldn't he sleep? He had been lying there for several hours, thinking about what he had seen and heard. Sometimes that would happen to him on a case. His head would take over, spinning, figuring, remembering. His head never cared if his body was tired. It just wouldn't quit.

Those bodies. He had only seen one—that was enough. He sat up, wondering if it was too late to find Earp and question him about the exact locations where the bodies were found. It had slipped his mind when he was jawing back and forth in their verbal duel. It probably wasn't professional to needle Earp like he did. Even if the marshal did seem set on giving it back to him. Lawmen just got on his nerves.

"Damn."

He took a few deep breaths but found he still was not sleepy. It had to be after midnight. He had heard the deputy marshals as they made their final rounds of the evening. He'd try to close his eyes. His head was spinning. Sounds in the night. Horses breathing, boards creaking, laughter from a bedroom too far away. He could hear the smith snoring downstairs in his room.

Raider listened for a long time before he sat up straight.

There was scratching downstairs. It stopped for a moment and then resumed. A squeaky hinge followed the scratching. Somebody was coming in through the stable's rear door.

His hand closed around the redwood handle of his Colt. He

thumbed back the hammer, wondering if the smith had a woman. Maybe she'd just go on into Walter's bed. Or maybe it wasn't a she. Maybe it was someone who had come to kill him.

Whoever it was had decided to climb the ladder to the loft.

Raider got to his feet, silently tiptoeing to the edge of the loft. He saw the dark shape moving up. Dropping to his belly, he waited for the intruder's hand to come slipping over onto the first rough board.

He grabbed the wrist and pressed the barrel of the Colt against the bushwhacker's forehead. "Don't move or I'll pull the trigger."

A woman gasped. "No—"

She struggled to get away, but he pulled her off the ladder, dangling her by the wrist over the forge below.

"Please," she said in a weak voice. "Don't—"

"Why shouldn't I drop you?" the big man offered. "You came t' kill me, didn't you? And you're gonna tell me who put you up to it."

"No. It's me. Kim. From the bathhouse!"

Raider lifted her onto the loft, dropping her into the straw. "What the hell are you doin' here?"

"I had to wait until my father was asleep," she replied. "I came to do what we wanted to do when you were in the tub."

"Stand up."

She peered up at him. "What?"

"I wanna make sure you ain't got no guns on you."

She obeyed him, rising to her feet. He didn't have to pat her down. Even in the shadows he could tell the Chinese woman was not carrying any weapons. He gave her a pat on the backside and urged her toward the ladder.

"Go on," he said. "You don't b'long here."

She pressed her body against his. "Please. Let me stay."

The smell of her hair was intoxicating.

"My father whips me," she went on. "And he makes me do things to him. I don't like it."

He allowed himself to hold her for just a few seconds. Then he pushed her away, looking into her face. "Kim—ain't that what you said your name was?—Kim, I gotta admit that you looked pretty good there today. But things are diff'rent since then. You gotta go. I cain't have any more trouble in this town, at least not till I finish what I came t' do."

"I love you," she said, trying to kiss him. "I saw you today and I knew I wanted you."

"Honey, you cain't stay." He shook her a little. "I mean it now."

She began to cry, which made it worse. She also rubbed the side of his leg, working her hand around to his crotch. Naturally he had sprung to life. What man wouldn't have stiffened under such circumstances?

So he gave in a little and let her linger. Before he knew it, they were naked and she was sitting on top of him, guiding his cock into her soft body. He knew that her father and Marshal Earp and the deputies could come in on them at any moment, arresting Raider and shipping him off to the territorial prison.

"Not inside of me," she whispered.

He rolled her over and got on top, driving his hips until his release began to rise.

"Not inside of me," she said again.

Raider pulled out, spraying his discharge all over her stomach.

He collapsed, rolling over, resting his head on the saddle.

Kim nuzzled into his chest, rubbing his stomach.

He wanted to say something but his eyes started to close. His last thought was to wonder if the girl might steal everything he had. But somehow it didn't seem to matter.

He slept soundly until the smith called him, warning that daybreak was close. When he sat up, he saw that all of his possessions were still there. The girl, however, had vanished, leaving only her telltale scent to assure him that she hadn't been a dream.

CHAPTER FOURTEEN

As the sun rose behind him, Raider galloped the sorrel mare west. In the early dawn light he could see vague outlines of the mountains ahead of him. The air had a hint of moisture and coolness, something that would disappear in a couple of hours, as soon as the sun got high enough.

He halted the mare and let her rest by a narrow stream that Raider believed to be the San Pedro River. According to the smithy's directions, the big man was on the right path. As soon as he got to the Fort Huachuca directional sign, he was to turn slightly south and ride for another couple of hours. So far the trail had not been hard to follow, as there was a fairly well-worn road. Plenty of prospectors and mining men had been through this particular part of the territory.

Raider mounted the sorrel again, crossing the San Pedro, keeping due west. When he saw the sign marking the way to the fort, he veered south and continued on at a lope. The mare didn't seem like she wanted to tire. He'd let her run until she decided to stop.

The road stretched out in front of him, connecting with side trails that all seemed to lead toward the mountains. By midmorning, the foothills were close enough to see the shaggy forests against the sky. The higher peaks were purple in the bright glow from the east.

He was making better time than he had hoped. If the smith was right, he'd soon come upon the fork in the road and the two signs that marked the different mining company trails. Sure enough, about an hour before midday, he reined up at the crossroads.

A bold, neatly painted sign pointed northwest, declaiming that the Ransom Ore Mines were only five miles away. A second sign pointed southwest, announcing that the Sierra Silver Company was eight miles in the other direction. Ransom was closer, but the dead man had been carrying a Sierra pay marker, so that seemed like the place to start.

Raider turned south, walking the mare for a while. The heat was rising on the plain, wavy lines that altered the view of the mountains. He rode the edge of the foothills, keeping his eyes trained to his right. Maybe the man who had killed Lucius McCabe was hiding in the ragged trees, peering down at him, waiting for a chance to put him off the case.

Even in the heat, the sorrel picked up her pace again, driving hard as the trail began to narrow. When the path became more rocky and marked with debris from the forest, he had to ease her into a walk again. And it turned out to be a good thing, especially when he came slowly around the corner and surprised the small party of Indians. Had he ridden up a little more quickly, the Indians might have been startled enough to take a shot at him.

But as it stood, they only settled back down around their campfire. Raider kept plodding toward them, taking note of their numbers. Seven of them. Apaches. What were they doing this far south? Maybe heading for Mexico. Some Indians did that, the way the northern tribes had gone up into Canada to get away from the white men.

One of the Apaches stood up as Raider got closer. They were older men, dark faces lined by years of fretting. Two of them were smoking pipes. The others just seemed to stare into the fire.

The Apache waved Raider by. Taking the hint, the big man rode around them, picking up into a trot when he had passed. No trouble at all. A few minutes later, he saw the sign pointing the way to Sierra Silver Company.

• • •

He forgot all about the Apaches when he started up the road toward the Sierra Silver mines. Rocks and fallen trees marked the trail, a path that had been hewn not long ago. Sierra seemed to be a fairly new operation.

As he ascended a rise, the ground leveled off and he caught his first glimpse of the mining operation and the company office. Three tunnels were being worked on the side of the steep slope that rose above the trees. A one-story cabin rested at the base of the slope, no doubt erected with trees that had been cut from the forest.

No one seemed to take notice of Raider as he rode toward the cabin. The miners were inside their holes and the office looked still, with the exception of a thin wisp of smoke from the chimney. Probably somebody was using a wood stove for cooking. Nobody needed heat on a day like this.

He guided the sorrel to the hitching post in front of the cabin. As he tied the reins, a short, pudgy man came out to greet him. He had long, gray sideburns and smoked a corncob pipe. He was dressed like any other prospector who had chipped away at a mountain.

The pudgy man extended his hand. "Howdy, stranger. What can I do for you?"

"I'm lookin' for the ramrod o' this outfit," Raider replied as he shook the man's hand. "You the owner?"

The man nodded, puffing out a little cloud of pipe smoke. "I'm the one. Name's Clairborn. Jack Clairborn."

"Call me Raider," the big man replied.

Clairborn nodded. "Raider. I'm afraid I can't help you out, partner. I'm hired up to the hilt. Got two brothers-in-law workin' for me and they both eat like a rich man's dog."

Raider studied the man, wondering if Clairborn's friendly nature was real or bogus. He appeared to be unthreatening, surely not the kind of man to torture someone to death. But Raider had to dig a little further.

"Ain't lookin' for work," he said. "I come t' talk t' you 'bout somethin' else."

Clairborn frowned a little. "All right. Would you like to come in and have a cup of coffee?"

Raider tipped his hat. "Much obliged."

He moved past the mining man, heading for the front door.

Clairborn moved to his right, reaching for something overhead. Raider turned sideways to watch his hands. Clairborn grabbed a cord and pulled it several times. A bell pealed overhead.

"Just tellin' my men that it's lunch time," he said. "I always give them a half hour break in the middle of the day. Some minin' bosses won't even give them a minute, but I figure a happy horse will pull a little harder."

Raider nodded. "Makes sense t' me. After you, Mr. Clairborn."

"Jack. Call me Jack."

Inside, the cabin seemed as harmless as its host. Clairborn offered Raider a chair and poured two cups of coffee. He apologized for not having real sugar. Raider told him molasses would do just fine.

When Clairborn was seated across the table from Raider, he eyed the big man as he torched his pipe. "Well," he offered, "you don't look like a lawman. Don't look like a miner, neither."

Raider wondered which way to go. Best to be honest with the man, he decided. See what the truth would give him.

"I'm a Pinkerton agent."

Clairborn nodded without showing any surprise. "Heard there was a Pinkerton in these parts. But last I knowed, he was locked up in the Tombstone jail. Would that be you?"

Raider nodded. "I'm not locked up no more."

Clairborn puffed on his pipe, watching the tall man. "So, what do you want with me, Mr. Pinkerton?"

Reaching into his shirt pocket, Raider took out the unused pay marker that had belonged to the late Lucius McCabe. "Found this on a man who turned up dead in the back alley of Tombstone. He never got t' cash it. The bank says he cashed the one the month afore last."

Clairborn lowered his head. "Lucius. I wondered what happened to him. Didn't figure he'd be dead, though."

"So he did disappear?" Raider asked.

Clairborn nodded. "Didn't think much of it when he never come back from town. That happens, you know. Miners who work for other people always think they can up and go start their own dig. They get a little grubstake and take off for the hills. Some of them make it, but most go bust."

It made sense that Clairborn would not think twice if a miner left without saying good-bye. And the pudgy man seemed to be sincere in his grief at learning the man was dead. Raider still wondered if it was all an act. He had seen some pretty unlikely villians who were able to fool him for a while. He usually caught on to them in the end, though.

Clairborn glared at him, his face reddening. "Hey, would this have anything to do with that body was found near here?"

Raider said he thought it did. He also mentioned the body that was found near the Ransom Ore Mines. He explained that the dead men, including Lucius McCabe, had all been tortured and killed by a brutal hand.

Clairborn shuddered. "Can't abide that sort of thing. Never have been one for killin'."

Raider leaned back in his chair, figuring an angle to get behind the facade of the mining man. "What can you tell me 'bout McCabe?"

Clairborn torched his pipe, thinking. "Well, he was a good worker. Came from Georgia, I believe. Not a young man. Maybe ten years older than you. But he managed to get around good. Never gave me much trouble, although the other workers complained that he was brash. Had a sharp tongue on him. Wasn't afraid to say his piece to anybody that would listen."

"Troublemaker?"

"No, not really." Clairborn sighed. "Dead. I can't believe it. I figured he'd turn up again, busted, lookin' for another chance to work up a grubstake. Who the hell would do such a thing?"

Raider pointed a finger at him. "That's what I hope you can help me find out. You willin'?"

Clairborn shifted in his chair. "Sure. Just tell me how I can help. I'll be happy to do anything I can."

"First, you can tell me where McCabe came from."

"That's easy. He was workin' over at Ransom before he come here."

Raider's brow fretted. "Ransom?"

"None other."

"Why'd he come over here?" the big man asked.

Clairborn blew out a puff of pipe smoke. "Got into a brawl with Ransom's ramrod. Man name of Taylor. Buck Taylor."

"And Ransom fired him?"

"No, I think Lucius walked. That was why I didn't think too much of it when he didn't show up here after I gave him the last pay marker. Figured he had just gone on his way."

Raider folded his hands, resting them on the table. "So McCabe usta work for Ransom."

Clairborn nodded. "Yep. Always bragged about how far back he went with Ransom. Said they had been in the war together."

"He was that old?"

"Yes, he was. Like I said, somewhere close to fifty. But he was a fit man. Worked hard. He was in good health."

"Wasn't in such good shape the last time I saw him," Raider offered.

Clairborn had broken a sweat.

Raider studied his ashen face. "You okay?"

The mining man shook his head. "I don't like this business at all. Killin' and such. I mean, I've had men killed in shoot-outs when they went into Tombstone, but this is different."

"A lot different," the big man replied. "How 'bout another cup o' coffee, Clairborn?"

As the man got up to retrieve the pot from the stove, Raider glanced around the cabin. Clairborn didn't even have a shotgun or a rifle on the wall. Raider wondered if he knew how to use a gun. Best not to get taken in by the man's charm and innocence. Not until a few more facts were clear.

"More molasses?" Clairborn asked as he filled the big man's cup.

Raider shook his head. "No. But I would like to ask another favor of you. It would help me a lot in this case."

"Name it," the miner rejoined.

"Can you take me t' the place where that body was found near here?"

Without hesitation, Clairborn put down the pot and started for the front door. "Come, Mr. Pinkerton. I'll take you there right now."

Raider stood up. "You mean you know where it is?"

"Of course," Clairborn replied. "I went out there myself when the damned thing was found. Took a look at that half-dug grave."

"I saw some Apaches near here today," the big man offered. "You know anythin' 'bout 'em?"

Clairborn's face slacked into a frown. "No."

"Reckon you better take your gun," Raider urged.

"Don't have one," Clairborn said.

Raider grimaced. "No gun?"

"Some of my men carry 'em, but I've never liked 'em much. Came out here from Illinois and we never carried weapons back there. Listen, I have to go saddle my mount. It will just take a minute.'

Raider waited by the hitching post as Clairborn went to get his mount. The miner seemed eager to help. Too eager. Raider checked his Colt, spinning the cylinder out of habit. Six rounds in place. He wondered if he was going to need them.

When they rode out, the Apaches were no longer to be seen. That didn't surprise Raider. But it didn't necessarily mean that they weren't still in the area. They might have been Mescaleros, up from Mexico for some unknown reason. Best to keep an ear turned to the wind.

Jack Clairborn led him east for a while. The miner shifted on the wide saddle of his mule, invoking one of Raider's superstitions. He had always been quick to trust a man who rode a mule, probably because his old partner had been partial to an ornery critter named Judith. Mescaleros had killed Judith. He felt funny now thinking about it.

As the sorrel wound down a narrow path that Clairborn found in the trees, Raider had to fight the urge to like the little man. Even if the miner had been cooperative so far, he was not above suspicion. When they dipped deeper in the scraggly forest, Raider lowered his hand to the butt of his Colt. What if Clairborn was leading him to a prearranged ambush?

"Just up here," the miner called back. "I know. When I heard about it, I came out here to look at the hole myself."

"Did you see the body?" Raider asked.

"No, can't say as I did."

They went on for a few hundred feet.

"There!" Clairborn said finally, reining in his mule.

Raider moved the sorrel next to him. He peered down at a shallow grave, less than four feet deep. He tipped back his Stetson and sighed.

Clairborn eyed him. "What's wrong?"

"The man who did this don't like diggin' deep graves," the big man replied. "Two prospectors found the body over by

Ransom 'cause a couple o' coyotes was diggin' it up."

Clairborn shivered. "Tough way to go. Havin' a coyote gnawin' out your guts. Glad it wasn't me."

"You wouldn't have cared. You'd be dead."

"Oh, that's right."

Raider dismounted, striding over by the shallow grave. Didn't the killer have enough sense to plant his victims deep enough to keep the varmints away from them? The man who done all this could not be stupid about such details. Three corpses. Raider had to wonder if there were any more victims on the murderer's list.

Clairborn was peering at him from the mule. "See anything?"

Raider toed a little reddish dirt into the grave. "Mebbe."

Red earth. The same hue that had been found in the hoofprints near the alley where the third body was discovered. That meant the same man had most likely done both murders. Or same men. Maybe there was more than one.

He circled the grave, searching for any signs that might give up a clue. There were too many tracks in the dirt. Probably every cowboy in the territory had been out to see it.

"I wonder if it could have been them Indians you saw?" Clairborn offered.

Raider shrugged. "Mebbe."

He had to consider the possibility that the killer might have wanted the dead bodies to be found. Maybe it was a warning to someone. What the hell was going on?

"Clairborn. How have things been 'tween the mines out this way?"

The pudgy man shrugged. "Fair to middlin'. We all leave each other alone mostly. Sometimes our crews fight it out in town, but that doesn't bother us too much."

Raider hunkered by the grave. "Any little men kickin' up a fuss?"

"You mean independents? No, not really. Hell, we can't take the whole mountain, so why do we care if a few grubstakers want to try their luck?"

"Nobody threatenin' anybody? Nobody pissed off?"

Clairborn's eyes narrowed a little. "I'll have you know, sir, that I have never said a cross word to anyone since I arrived in this territory from Illinois. Do you hear me, sir?"

"I hear you."

Clairborn gasped when Raider leaped down into the hole.

"Don't worry, Jack," the big man said with a smile. "Nobody was ever buried here, so it ain't really a grave."

As the miner watched in disbelief, Raider went around the edge of the hole, running his finger through the dirt. When that turned up nothing, he bent down and felt the bottom of the hole, sifting through the dirt with his open hands. He finally hit something that rolled out into the light, reflecting a brassy hue in the sun.

"Well, this looks interestin'."

He picked up a brass button and dusted the red dirt from it, revealing the initials *U.S.* Same as the first one. Things were coming together but he still wasn't any closer to an answer.

"Look at this, Clairborn."

He tossed the button in the air. The miner managed to catch it in his right hand. He studied it for a moment and nodded.

"Ever seen one like it afore?" Raider asked.

"Yes, sir. On the coat of a Union soldier."

The big man came out of the grave. "Fight in the war, did you?"

"Ran a riverboat along the Mississippi."

Raider looked at him. "For which side?"

Clairborn chuckled. "Depends on what time of the war you're talkin' about. I carried both sides, blue and gray, and supplies for both. I seen these buttons on the sleeves of blue coats."

"Officers?"

Clairborn nodded. "Glad those times are over. Didn't care much for war. Glad to be west now."

Raider swung into the saddle of the sorrel mare. "Seems you do okay no matter what line you go into, Clairborn."

The miner glared at him. "What's that s'posed to mean?"

"Nothin'. Thanks for bringin' me out here. I think I'm on the right trail now. But where it's gonna end, I cain't say."

Clairborn looked down at the grave. "Well, if you can put an end to such shenanigans, then I'm happy to be of some help."

Raider leaned on his saddlehorn. "I hope you told me ever'thin' you know 'bout this, Clairborn."

The miner's head snapped back indignantly. "I've not held back a word, sir. And I wouldn't if you paid me."

Raider pointed up the trail. "You lead the way out."

Clairborn hesitated. "What are you goin' to do next?"

"Mebbe talk to some o' your men. Mebbe go over t' Ransom Ore an' have a talk with Levon Ransom."

Clairborn seemed to pale somewhat. "Levon Ransom ain't a man to be took lightly, Pinkerton. He can be meaner than a copperhead."

"So can I."

"No, I'm not joshin'. Watch your step around Ransom."

Raider's eyes narrowed. "Listen, Clairborn, if you've got somethin' t' say agin Ransom, tell me now afore I go in there alone."

"No—I—"

"You think he had somethin' t' do with those three killin's? Speak out if you're hidin' somethin'."

"Ain't hidin' nothin'," Clairborn replied.

He urged his mule up the trail.

Raider fell in behind him, walking the mare. Clairborn hadn't bristled until Ransom's name came up. He was the second one to tell Raider to watch his step around Levon Ransom. Raider hadn't even met the man yet and he was already forming on opinion of him. Best to wait and make his own judgments. Sometimes things just weren't as they seemed.

He rode for a while before he looked over his shoulder.

Clairborn glanced back at him. "Everything okay, Pinkerton?"

Raider motioned him forward. "Just a squirrel."

They rode on for a while, until they reached the sign that pointed the way to the Sierra dig.

Raider reined up, calling to Clairborn.

The miner looked back again. "You comin' to talk to my men?"

Raider pointed north. "I think I'll ride on t' the Ransom mines. I'll come back this way if I need you."

"Suit yourself," Clairborn replied. "I'll be right here if you want my help. Like I said, I got no secrets."

Raider almost believed him. He turned the sorrel north and spurred her along the trail. He wanted to get away from Clairborn in a hurry. They were being followed and Raider was anxious to see who the trailing rider would come after.

The rider followed Raider, which was going to make it harder to set a trap. If the trailer had gone after Clairborn, then the big man could have caught him and surprised him from behind. But he had chosen to follow Raider, which meant that a good trick was in order.

Raider wondered who was after him. Maybe the Apaches had sent one brave to do away with the threat to their movements. The whole business stunk of some Indian cult. Tortured bodies and shallow graves.

What if there was more than one Indian? Maybe there was an ambush up ahead. Raider remembered a spot where the trees hung low over the trail. They might be waiting for him there.

Raider suddenly felt hot under the collar. He had only been on the case for a couple of days, but he was already growing impatient. Best just to take care of his pursuer before any damage was done.

He reached a place on the trail where the land rose to one side. Above on the rise was a clump of small boulders. Not a bad place to hide. He dismounted, took his Winchester from the scabbard and slapped the sorrel on the rump so the animal would continue on without him in the saddle.

Running up the slope, he slid behind the boulders and waited. The rider wasn't far behind, so he levered the rifle, jacking a cartridge into the chamber. The rider came into sight almost soon enough to hear the echoing rattle of the rifle lever.

He wasn't an Indian. Tall in the saddle, clad in a black suit. Rifle on the sling ring of his saddle. Side arm. He plodded forward on a strong black gelding.

Raider took aim in front of the horse. He could have jumped the rider but this was easier. He hoped it would work.

When the rider was just below him on the trail, he let off one round that kicked up dirt in front of the gelding. Just as Raider had hoped, the horse reared, throwing the unsuspecting rider out of the saddle. The man landed on his ass with a thump.

Raider came out of the rocks, stepping down the incline.

The rider, who was gasping for air, tried to go for his side arm. Raider reached him in time to put the rifle in his face. The man hesitated, gaping at the one-eyed bore of the Winchester.

"I wouldn't move," the big man told him.

"Don't shoot. It's me."

Raider couldn't see the man's face in the shadow of his hat brim. He knocked the hat off with the barrel of the Winchester. He recognized him immediately. One of Earp's deputies.

"You dumb son of a buck! What the hell you doin' out here followin' me? Huh? I oughta shoot you right b'tween the eyes."

The deputy pleaded for his life. "No, I didn't want to do it, Pinkerton. Marshal Earp ordered me to follow you."

Raider lowered the barrel of the rifle. "Shit. You dad-blamed tinhorn lawmen are always gettin' in my way. I've a good mind t' drop this case right here an' now."

"No!" The deputy tried to smile. "Please. If Wyatt thinks I messed this up, he'll—"

Raider turned away from him, striding toward the black gelding which had stopped up the trail.

"Hey," the deputy cried, "that's my mount!"

Raider swung into the saddle of the black. "Not anymore. I'll leave it tied up the trail when I find my own horse."

"What am I supposed to tell Wyatt?"

"Tell him next time he gets in my way I'm gonna drop this whole thing in his lap. Comprende?"

He didn't wait for an answer. He dug along the trail until he found his mount nibbling on a tuft of dried grass. Then he changed horses and rode hard to the north, toward the Ransom Ore Mines and Levon Ransom.

CHAPTER FIFTEEN

By late afternoon, Raider had reached the sign that pointed the five mile route to the Ransom Ore Mines. When he reined up by the post, he peered east, toward a cloud of dust that barely stirred in the still, hot air. Probably a wagon, or a buggy. He waited for a while, resting his mount, watching as the vehicle drew closer.

It was a buggy coming toward him. Doc Bascomb's buggy. The old boy was making his call rather late, Raider thought. He waved until the doctor saw him by the signpost.

The old gentleman reined back and tipped his hat. "Are you just getting here too, sir?"

Raider nodded. "You're a mite late yourself."

Bascomb frowned. "It was that friend of yours."

Raider grimaced. "Friend?"

"Holliday. He overdid it with that tincture I gave him and almost killed his fool self."

Raider shook head. "He's somethin', ain't he?"

"You comin' or goin'?" Bascomb asked.

"Comin'. I was over t' Sierra Silver. That Clairborn seems

like a good man, but sometimes it's hard t' tell. A man can hide some pretty bad things inside hisself."

"More than you know, Mr. Pinkerton."

Raider gestured toward the hills ahead of them. "You know the way?"

Bascomb nodded. "I do."

Raider swung into the saddle of the sorrel. "Take the lead, Doc. I'll be right b'side you."

The good doctor was eyeing the big man. "Be careful with this bunch, sir. They're not to be trifled with."

"Neither am I, Doc. Neither I am."

Long shadows fell over the hills as they approached the encampment of the Ransom Ore mines. The whole place looked dirtier than the Sierra dig. Baked, splintered log dwellings rested in the bare patches of forest that had provided the logs. The road sloped upward toward a larger lodge that seemed to serve as the offices for the operation.

Raider eased the mare even with the buggy seat. "Don't anybody ever sweep up 'round this place?"

Bascomb chuckled. "Ransom's going to love you, Raider."

"Know him good, d' you?"

"Not really," the doctor replied.

Raider was going to ask him something else, but the unmistakable threat of rifle levers resounded above them.

"Hold it right there."

Raider's hand fell reflexively toward his Colt.

"No!" Bascomb said. "There's four of them. On the rooftops of the bunkhouses. And there, behind those rocks."

Raider stopped and put his hands back on the horn of his saddle. No point in going against overwhelming odds. Besides, it was natural to have guards on duty, especially with an operation that had a lot of silver on hand. Why hadn't Clairborn posted guards? he wondered.

Bascomb waved to the sentries. "It's all right, boys."

"He with you, Doc?"

Bascomb nodded. "Yep. Came to see Mr. Ransom."

"Go on up," the sentry replied.

Bascomb smiled, waved, and then called, "What's the matter? Is Bubba's bad leg bothering him again?"

"No, it's Buck Taylor. He's hurt his hand."

Bascomb blanched, his face going completely white.

"You all right?" Raider asked.

Bascomb urged his horse forward. Raider fell in next to the buggy, watching the old man's face. The doctor seemed to be shaking.

"Doc—"

"It's Taylor," the old man replied. "I don't like him. You'll see, if you get to meet him."

They continued up the road until they reached the big lodge at the summit of the hill. Doc Bascomb reined back on his buggy horse, stopping close to the plank door of the cabin. Raider swung out of the saddle, tying his mount to the back of the buggy.

Doc Bascomb was climbing down as the man came out of the lodge to meet them. He was tall, blond, rugged. He wore a black suit that didn't seem to be big enough for him. Raider figured he was the kind of man who could make things tough in a fair fight. But then he saw that the man's right hand was bandaged.

The man started to speak to Doc Bascomb, but he stopped cold when his eyes fell on Raider. His wolfish eyes narrowed. Raider tipped his hat and tried to smile.

"Who's this?" the man asked, nodding at Raider.

Doc Bascomb tried to play peacemaker. "He's come to speak to Mr. Ransom," the doctor replied. "His name is Raider."

"What's he want with Mr. Ransom?"

"Personal business," Raider offered, never wavering.

"This is Buck Taylor," the doctor said.

Raider had figured as much. They didn't shake hands. Raider couldn't remember the last time he had been in a good fight. Although he had to wonder if Taylor had enough guts to scrap with a busted paw.

"Mr. Ransom doesn't want to see anybody," Taylor said.

Raider ignored him. "How'd you hurt your hand, Taylor?"

"I hit it with a hammer."

Doc Bascomb stood between them, wondering if he was going to get caught in the middle of a ruckus. "Gentlemen, there's no need for this. Levon Ransom is a reasonable man. I'm sure if he—"

"Mr. Ransom won't see anybody today," Taylor repeated. "Especially no Pinkerton."

Raider bristled a little.

"Yeah, I know who you are—"

"Buck!"

Taylor turned back toward the door. "Mr. Ransom, there's—"

"I'll see him," came the voice from the lodge. "Let the doctor tend to your hand."

Taylor glared at Raider. "I'll see you again."

"I'm lookin' forward to it, Taylor."

Bascomb grabbed Buck Taylor's injured hand.

"Oww!"

"Mebbe we can ride back t'gether, Doc."

Bascomb nodded.

Raider moved past him, unaware of how prophetic his statement would be.

The lodge was dim and cool inside. Raider had to wait for his eyes to adjust. The place smelled like tobacco and bacon. He could barely make out the shape that sat in the corner, smoking a hand-rolled cigarette.

"So, you're the Pinkerton." The voice was cool and dark, like the lodge.

"Call me Raider."

"Call me Mr. Ransom."

"Okay."

The dark shape struck a match and torched the end of a tallow candle. Raider saw the face as the candle swelled in a circle of light. He was a small man, which accounted for the presence of a man like Taylor. Ransom needed a bodyguard.

"Why have you come here?" Ransom asked.

Trace of the old south in his lilting accent. He lit a cigarette off the candle, puffing it to life to replace the other one. He was older than Raider but younger than Doc Bascomb. Worn face. Deep-set eyes.

"I'd like t' talk t' you, Mr. Ransom."

"About the two bodies that were found out this way?"

He had said it offhandedly, as if the lives of those two men had meant nothing to him.

Raider frowned a little, his eyes narrowing. "You seem t'

know a whole lot 'bout it, Ransom. Mebbe you have somethin' you'd like t' tell me."

"I know nothing about it. Nothing at all."

"Then mebbe you'd like t' know this. There was a third man killed in Tombstone. His name was Lucius McCabe."

No response from the man in the chair, except the cigarette smoke that curled around his head.

"McCabe," Raider repeated, "you ever hear that name afore?"

Ransom's shoulders shrugged forward. "Should I?"

"McCabe worked for you," Raider replied. "But then he left an' went over t' work for Clairborn at Sierra Vista. We found a pay marker from there in his pants pocket."

Ransom just sat there.

"McCabe usedta brag 'bout bein' in the army with you, Ransom. Claimed you an' him was big buddies."

"Are you asking me to dignify that statement with an answer?"

Raider nodded. "It might set a few things right."

Ransom flicked ash on the floor. "Wyatt Earp has no jurisdiction out here. And he also doesn't have the guts to come in person. He has to hire a piecework lawman. A bounty hunter."

"I ain't the important man, Ransom. I'm lookin' at you. And you don't seem too willin' t' help out. Mebbe you got somethin' t' hide."

Ransom laughed. "That could be. But listen to this. Yes, I did know McCabe. And yes, we were in the army together. The gray army, sir. Sons of Dixie. The Confederate States of America."

"That was the side that lost," the big man rejoined.

Ransom glared up at him. "You sound as if you come from south of the Mason-Dixon line."

"Arkansas, if it's any o' your business."

"Did you fight for Dixie?"

"Never got the chance," Raider replied. "I was too young."

"I'm sorry to hear that."

Raider shifted to his feet. "Let's get back t' bus'ness, Ransom."

"*Mister* Ransom."

"Levon!"

Ransom smiled slightly. "Touché, Pinkerton."

"What you know 'bout McCabe?"

Ransom shrugged. "He served with me at Andersonville."

"The prison?"

"Was there ever any other? Those were some of the darkest days of my life." His voice seemed to sadden. "I shall never forget that horror. And I was on the side of the captor."

Raider didn't want to stray off the subject at hand. "Why did McCabe leave you t' go work for Clairborn?"

"He wanted higher wages. To be made foreman. But I said no. So he took his talents elsewhere."

That sounded reasonable enough, but Raider still had his doubts. "Two more men were killed just like McCabe."

Ransom glared at him. "What do you mean 'just like' McCabe?"

Raider thought he saw an opening. "Tortured. Hacked up, split with knives. The one who did it even took a hatchet t' McCabe's knees. Sliced him up pretty good."

Ransom's shudder seemed genuine.

"Yeah, McCabe was shot—"

"No more," Ransom said.

"But there will be more," Raider insisted. "More death, more torture. That's why I have t' stop it."

"I can't help you," Ransom pleaded. "I can't."

Raider pointed a finger at him. "Tell me what you know, Ransom. What 'bout McCabe?"

"Nothing more than I've told you. I knew him. He came to work for me. He left willingly and I haven't seen him since."

"Did he come out here with anyone?"

Ransom shook his head. "No, not that I know of."

"Have any men turned up missin'?"

"I don't know!" Ransom cried. "I don't know."

He put his head in his hands and began to whimper. Raider wasn't sure what to do. He never saw that many men who came right out and cried. What the hell had gotten to Ransom?

"I'd like permission t' talk t' your crew, Ransom. I'd like t' speak t' your foreman."

The man glanced up at him. "Why?"

"T' see who he's hired an' fired. T' see if any men left without takin' their belongin's. I'd like t' figger out the names o' the other two men who were killed. And I cain't do that without a downright investigation. I gotta turn over ever' rock in this territory."

Ransom seemed to be recovering a little. "I don't know if I should let you. You don't have any jurisdiction here."

"There's a gover'ment in this terr'tory," the big man reminded him. "It may not be much, but if you cause trouble, I can see to it that somebody comes back here t' take up where I quit."

"Then why don't you do that, Pinkerton!"

The voice had come from behind him.

Raider glanced over his shoulder to see Buck Taylor standing there in the doorway. "I was just talkin' t' your boss here."

Taylor stepped into the room holding his bandaged hand in front of him. "You're through talkin'. The doc is waitin' for you outside."

Raider looked back at the man in the chair. "What you gotta say 'bout this, Mr. Ransom.?

Before Ransom could speak, Taylor moved around between them. "Mr. Ransom is tired, Pinkerton. So why don't you just clear out?"

Raider smiled, pointing at the fresh bandage. "Doc Bascomb did a good job on you, Taylor."

Taylor's wolfish eyes turned to narrow slits. "You'd better go. And make it quick."

"Two nights ago, I shot at a man in the alley out b'hind the stable. He was the one caught torturin' Lucius McCabe. The one who put a pistol t' McCabe's head an' pulled the trigger."

"So?" Taylor replied, scowling. "What of it?"

"I could've shot him in the hand," Raider offered. "Where the hell were you two nights ago, Taylor?"

"You son of a bitch. I oughta—"

Ransom held out his hand. "Enough."

Raider looked back at the small dark man. "The truth is gonna float t' the top sooner or later, Ransom. If your man here is locked up in somethin' bad, I'm gonna find out in my own time."

"Two nights ago I was right here with Mr. Ransom," Taylor said.

"That's true?" Raider challenged.

Ransom nodded. "Yes. Now perhaps you should go, Pinkerton. And don't come back."

Raider eased toward the door, keeping his face toward them. He wanted to keep an eye on Taylor's good hand. He had a feeling he had landed right in the middle of the rattler's nest. And he wanted to get the hell out before one of them struck him.

Doc Bascomb was staring wide-eyed at Raider when he came out of the cabin. "What the devil were you doing in there?"

Raider waved him off. "Let's ride first. I'll tell you all 'bout it when we've cleared this camp."

He untied the sorrel and swung into the saddle.

Doc Bascomb turned the buggy and started down the hill. Raider fell in beside him. They passed the sentries, who waved them through.

"Ransom's got some firepower," Raider said in a low voice.

"And you've got them all stirred up," the doctor replied.

"Just keep movin'."

They rode for a while, putting the encampment behind them.

"I wonder if Taylor came out t' watch us go?" Raider said.

Doc Bascomb shook his head. "I don't like this one bit."

They kept on, riding into dull shadows as the sun sank lower behind them. Not long till dark. Birds were on the wing and the air smelled like fresh earth. Raider turned to look over his shoulder.

Doc Bascomb did the same. "You don't think he'd send somebody after you, Raider?"

The big man shrugged. "Hard t' say. But Ransom is hidin' somethin'."

"What makes you say that?"

Raider spun back, looking straight ahead. "Well, Ransom said he knew that man who was killed in Tombstone."

"What man?"

"Name was McCabe. Say, did Earp have you come an' look at the body?"

Bascomb shook his head. "I only look at the live ones."

"Speakin' o' live ones," Raider said, "what did Taylor's hand wound look like? How bad was it?"

Bascomb sighed. "It was a deep gash. Looked like he cut it on a butchers knife or something like that."

Raider grimaced. "It wasn't a bullet wound? Like somebody had shot him through the hand?"

"No, not like any bullet hole I've ever seen."

Raider thought about it for a second. "I could've grazed him."

"What?"

Raider looked over his shoulder again. He wondered how far down Ransom had placed his sentries. Were they still in sight?

Bascomb glanced sideways at the Pinkerton who rode so tall in the saddle. "You have a plan, don't you?"

Raider turned forward again. "There's somethin' goin' on up there, Bascomb. I ain't sure what it is yet, but it could have somethin' t' do with all the silver that's been comin' outta this place."

Bascomb wiped sweat from his forehead. "I don't like this, sir. I'd advise you to leave Ransom alone."

"Just keep movin', Doc."

They rode until the sun was almost gone. Raider reined up, prompting the doctor to halt the buggy. The big man turned to look back. There was no way any of Ransom's guards could see them now.

"You're going back, aren't you?" Bascomb asked.

Raider lifted his Colt from the holster, checking the cylinders to make sure he was ready. "I gotta go back there, Bascomb. I gotta find out what's goin' on 'round here."

The doctor shook his head. "I won't have any part of it."

"I don't expect you to, Doc." He lowered the Colt back into his holster. "If I don't come back by t'morrow, tell Earp what I done."

"You consarned fool, you'd better—"

"Adios!"

He spurred the sorrel and drove hard to retrace his trail.

Riding straight into the encampment was not a good idea; not with Buck Taylor around. He'd have to slip in under the cloak of night, sneaking around like a weasel in a chicken coop. Gazing up the shadowed slope, he wondered if he should be traipsing around in the dark.

At the base of the thin forest, he found a place to tie up the sorrel. He was far enough down the hill that the mare would probably not be discovered by any of Ransom's men. How many sentries had he counted? Four. And there were miners too. Outnumbered to beat all hell.

Reaching for a handful of mud, he smeared it on to darken his face. No need to be a hero on this particular night. Just slip in, see what he could see and get the hell out. If he didn't find anything, he could start watching the place from a distance, maybe even use a telescope glass.

Tonight he was going in.

He followed the road, keeping close to the edge of the trees. He was halfway up when he heard a rider galloping pell-mell down the path. Raider lunged into the trees, landing on his belly.

The rider sped by without slowing.

Raider sat up, listening, afraid that the rider might see his mount at the bottom of the incline.

But the horse kept pounding until it disappeared into the night.

"Didn't die that time," he said under his breath.

As he made it to the crest of the first rise, he saw lights ahead of him. Again he fell back into the shadows, watching. The miners had come down from their holes. They lined up in front of a cabin that seemed to serve as a mess hall. Torches burned overhead as the miners got a plate of stew and a hunk of bread.

Good, Raider thought, they were occupied with dinner. He turned and gazed through the trees. He figured he could wind his way between the trunks, slipping into the camp to a better vantage point. He remembered that there were cabins on both sides of the road. Maybe he could hide under a window and listen for a while. Not exactly a straight-on way of dealing with this case, but sometimes you just had to sneak around.

Slowly he stepped between the trees, trying not to make any noise. When he had gone a hundred feet, he saw the dark shape of a building ahead of him. One of the miners' cabins. It was pitch black inside. No torches burning.

Easing to the edge of the woods, he saw that he would have to cover some bare ground if he intended to make it to the cabin. He glanced at the miners, who were still busy eating. His own stomach had begun that steady churning that came with action.

He took a deep breath. He'd have to run, stay low. Either that or turn back. What the hell was he doing here anyway?

No, he'd go on. Stay by the cabin for a while. Listen. Then wait until everybody got settled for a night's sleep. He could leave or even steal up to the main house and spy on Ransom.

Damn it all, why did he have to sneak around? Because it took a sneak to catch one. Ransom and Taylor sure as the devil seemed to be up to something. He thought about the dead man and the other tortured souls.

Best to stay low and keep moving.

He was halfway across the open ground when he heard the voice.

"Hey, what the hell are you doin'?"

He went belly down, freezing in the warm night air.

"Hey, you!"

His hand went to the butt of his Colt. He wondered how many of them he would have to kill. He could always try running.

Somebody from the mining camp called out, "What the hell do you want, Harvey?"

A voice from the dark replied, "Save some of that stew for us."

"Ah, you boys don't really work."

The miners laughed.

"I ain't eatin' beans just because you ate all the stew."

They all laughed again.

Raider got up, running to the edge of the cabin. He breathed hard, leaning against the wall of logs. He had not drawn his Colt.

Something moved in front of him. A man walked to the edge of the woods and relieved himself. He turned and went back to his dinner without seeing Raider in the shadows. The big man figured he had better get to the rear of the cabin. He moved toward the corner of the structure.

As he slid around to the back of the cabin, he heard the deep voice.

"That's far enough."

He was reaching for his Colt when the second man dropped from the roof, landing beside him.

The man put the bore of a pistol against Raider's ear. "Don't move, big cowboy. There's a rifle on you too."

"Hey," Raider said, "I ain't—"

"That's right, boy, you ain't anythin'!"

The rifle seemed to come out of nowhere.

The second man lifted the Colt from Raider's holster.

"Let's take him up to see Taylor," the rifle man said.

The man with the pistol agreed that was a good idea.

They ushered Raider into the torchlight, where all the miners jeered and hollered at the big man.

"You boys got this all wrong," Raider offered.

The rifleman hit him in the shoulder with the butt of his Winchester. "Just keep movin', Pinkerton."

Somebody from the crowd cried: "Hey, he's the Pinkerton!"

The miners fell in behind him as they pushed Raider toward Ransom's lodge. Some of them grabbed torches to light the way. Raider had to feel pretty stupid, especially when he saw Buck Taylor coming out of the lodge.

"Well," Taylor said, "I thought I told you to hightail it, Pinkerton."

Raider gave his best coyote grin. "Yeah, an' I reckon I shoulda listened."

Taylor was leering at him. Raider had wondered how it would be to scrap with the tall, wolf-eyed man. Now it looked like he was going to get his chance to find out firsthand.

CHAPTER SIXTEEN

The miners circled around Raider. Buck Taylor came through the line of men, only to have the line close behind him. Raider was trapped inside the circle. He figured there were at least twenty of them surrounding him. Bad odds, even if he had been allowed to keep his Colt. He tried to look brave, but his gut was churning.

Buck Taylor glared at him. "You know, I could shoot you for sneakin' around our camp like this and nobody, not even the marshal, would say a word about it, Pinkerton."

Raider shrugged. "Mebbe. But then again, mebbe not. Earp knows I came out here and—"

"Earp is a fool," Taylor replied. "And so are you."

Raider figured he wasn't in any position to disagree. The miners echoed Taylor's sentiments. They were hoping for some sort of scrap. Or maybe a lynching. The circle tightened around him.

"What the hell are you looking for anyway?" Taylor asked.

Raider wondered if this might be the opportunity to state his case. "I'm lookin' for a killer," he replied, fixing his gaze on the men around him. "Three bodies have been found. One

124

of 'em is a miner just like y'all. Man name of Lucius McCabe."

Taylor scowled at the big man. "Shut up!"

But his point had been made.

Somebody from the crowd said, "Lucius ain't dead. He went to work for Clairborn."

"Yeah," another miner rejoined, "he went to work for Clairborn."

Raider nodded, his black eyes reflecting the torchlight. "That's right. He did work for Clairborn. Until I found him dead in an alley in Tombstone. Now he's buried up on Boot Hill."

"He's lyin'!" Taylor cried.

"McCabe had his pay marker in his pocket," Raider went on. "Never even got the chance t' cash it."

A man with a torch leaned in a little. "Clairborn did pay with markers," he said. "Lucius told me when I saw him in town."

Taylor waved the man back. "Don't listen to him. This Pinkerton here is just tryin' to cause trouble."

"The trouble has already been caused," Raider went on. "Besides McCabe, there's been two other men killed."

"Were they miners?" somebody called.

Raider exhaled defeatedly. "That I cain't say. But that's what I come up here t' find out. Two of the bodies were found in these parts. One over by Sierra, the other one right near here."

That bit of news caused a stir in the miners.

Raider was feeling better until Buck Taylor waved his bandaged hand. "All of you, shut up! Don't listen to this idiot. Hell, you know how Pinks can cause trouble!"

"They are listenin', Buck."

Taylor pointed at him with the wounded paw. "Shut your trap, Pinkerton."

Raider decided to play to the buzzing crowd of men. "I shot at the man who killed Lucius McCabe. I hit him too. I found blood in the alley where I was chasin' him."

"That's enough!" Taylor cried through clenched teeth.

Raider pointed to Taylor's bandaged hand. "Why don't you ask Buck here how he hurt his hand? Maybe that'd—"

Taylor swung with his good hand, striking a blow that

barely grazed Raider's chin. Raider eased back a little, anticipating the next punch. Taylor had to regain his balance,
squaring his shoulders.

"Get him, Buck!" came the cry from the crowd.

Taylor hesitated, glaring in the torchlight.

"He's only got one hand!" somebody said.

Raider eyed Ransom's bodyguard. "Yeah, you only got one
hand, Buck. Don't seem like it would be fair for me an' you t'
mix it up. Why don't I come back when you're feelin' a mite
better?"

A thin smile broke over Taylor's lips. "You ain't goin'
nowhere, Pinkerton. Not until I say so."

"You talk mighty big with your boys t' back you up,"
Raider offered.

"They'd jump you right now if I told them to," Taylor
replied. "And I just might tell them to."

Raider glanced around at the angry miners. "Twenty to
one. Now that seems like a coward's odds."

Somebody cried, "Buck ain't no coward!"

Raider didn't like the way the miners were closing in. They
could smell the blood. And Taylor was their man, not Raider.
The Pinkerton had invaded their camp looking for trouble.
And now he had found it.

The line of men parted behind Taylor. A smaller man came
into the torchlight. Levon Ransom stepped up next to Buck
Taylor.

"What the devil is going on here, Buck?" Then he saw
Raider standing there in the middle of the circle. "Oh, I see.
The Pinkerton has returned. That was a big mistake, Pinker-
ton."

"I'm beginnin' t' see that," Raider replied.

Ransom grinned. "Cocky. You should be taught some
manners."

"We were just about to start his lesson," Taylor said.

Ransom nodded. "That might be a good idea. We could
teach this ape a thing or two about honor."

Ransom started to back away.

"Honor!" Raider cried.

The miner hesitated, his face slacking into a frown.

"You don't know shit about honor!" Raider cried. "Is it
honorable to have all your men beat me to a pulp?"

Ransom pointed a finger at him. "You're the interloper, Pinkerton!"

Even though he had no idea what an interloper was, Raider still pleaded his case. "I'm just an honest d'tective tryin' t' do my job, Ransom."

"Shut up!" Taylor cried. "You can't talk to Mr. Ransom like that."

"I'll talk any way I see fit, Buck. Hell, you boys don't know the first thing 'bout honor or manners. I come in here t' ask a few simple questions 'bout men that've been killed an' nobody wants me t' know the truth. And as long as I been in this line o' work, it always seems like men who want t' hide the truth are the ones who never lend a hand. Like you, Ransom. How come you don't want me to know the truth?"

Ransom just stood there, his face slowly spreading into a wry smile. "The truth, eh? Is that what you want? Buck, why don't you tell this man the truth as we see it."

Taylor also smiled. "Truth is, Pinkerton, you got a whippin' comin' to you and you're gonna get it before you leave this camp."

Raider chortled, trying to keep up a brave front. "Twenty t' one. I reckon the pride of Dixie has changed some when it comes t' honor, eh, Ransom?"

The mining man moved toward him a little, staring at the big man from Arkansas. Raider had gotten to him with the crack about the pride of Dixie. No self-respecting rebel could stand there and have his honor attacked. Ransom was no different.

"We're gonna take him apart," Taylor said. "Boys—"

Raider braced for the onslaught.

Ransom raised his hand. "No. Wait."

Taylor squinted at his boss. "Mr. Ransom, we—"

"Just wait," the small man said.

He circled Raider, then came back to face him again. Ransom seemed to be thinking. He looked at Taylor's bandaged hand, rubbing his chin.

"Buck is correct about one thing, Pinkerton. You do have a whipping in store for you. After all, you did trespass on my property at night. Why, I could have shot you and even that idiot marshal in Tombstone couldn't have said a word to me."

Raider shrugged. "Mebbe."

"No doubt about it," Ransom replied. "But you see, you are right about something as well. Twenty to one, and it's more like twenty-five to one, cannot really be considered a gentleman's fight."

"Aw, hell," came the voice from the crowd, "let's get him, Mr. Ransom."

Raider saw the dark shapes of the miners in his peripheral vision. They wanted blood. His blood. He wondered if they would actually kill him.

Ransom held up his hand to silence them. "Consider it, my friends," he said to his crew. "Twenty-five to one. How would you feel if it was you standing there where the Pinkerton is? No, you wouldn't like it one bit."

Raider grimaced at Ransom. "Don't tell me you've up an' switched over t' my side?"

"Hardly." He smiled a little. "But the fact remains, as Buck said, you can't leave here unpunished. And even if you don't deserve a fair fight, since you are blood of the South, I feel inclined to give you a chance against Buck here."

Taylor scowled at his boss. "I can't fight him with one hand, Mr. Ransom. That wouldn't be fair."

A cruel expression came over the miner's face. "No, but if we were to take one of the Pinkerton's hands away, it would be an even match."

Raider felt his stomach diving off a cliff. "You mean you're gonna cut off one o' my hands? Hell, I'd just as soon take my chances with all these goons you got here."

"Who you callin' goons!" came the angry reply.

"We ain't goons! Let us get him, Mr. Ransom."

"Yeah, we'll teach him a thing or two."

Ransom held up his hands to quiet them. "He's going to get his just reward, my friends. But we'll do it my way."

Raider wondered if he should go ahead and make his move. Just turn tail and try to run through the weakest man in the circle. Make it to the dark trees and find his mount. They could shoot him in the back, but if he ran fast enough, he might be able to get away.

Ransom gestured to one of the men in the circle. "Get a rope and tie one of his hands behind his back."

Buck Taylor grimaced at his boss. "What the devil—"

Ransom shrugged. "It's the only way."

The man moved behind Raider with the rope. "Which hand, Mr. Ransom?"

"Well, since Buck's right hand is busted, then make it the Pinkerton's right. That okay with you, Pinkerton?"

Raider sighed, putting his right hand behind him. "Don't seem like I got a whole lotta choice."

Taylor didn't seem to like his boss's idea. "Mr. Ransom, this ain't right. I mean—"

Ransom waved him off. "You're both going to fight with one hand, Buck. It's the only fair way. And Buck. You better take him."

Raider felt his wrist being lashed to his gun belt. "Are you gonna tie Taylor's hand b'hind his back, Ransom?"

The miner shook his head. "No, you'll just have to live with it, Pinkerton. This is your only chance. Take it or leave it."

Raider figured he'd take it. The man who had tied his hand moved away. Buck Taylor started to circle, holding his left hand out. He could still get leverage with his right arm, even if it was bandaged.

"Get him, Buck!"

"Show him what you got, Buck!"

The miners raised their torches, lighting the ring. Ransom stepped back to join his men. They closed in, making the circle smaller.

Raider regarded his foe. Taylor had the same wolfish expression on his face. Raider figured he would come after him in a hurry. A hungry wolf couldn't wait to draw blood.

Sure enough, Taylor made a lunge, leading with his left fist. But the blow was awkward and Raider sidestepped the punch. Taylor spun past him but easily regained his balance.

Raider grinned at his opponent. "This ain't gonna be as easy as you thought, Buck."

"You son of a bitch!"

The miners hollered for their man as he rushed Raider. The big man's left arm tensed but the reflexive blow did not materialize. Instead, Taylor tackled him, sending him into the dirt.

"Buck's on him now!"

"Hit him, Buck!"

Raider told himself to use his left, the free hand. Taylor was on top of him, slapping with both hands, even the ban-

daged palm of his right. Raider felt the pain in the arm that
was trapped behind him. He tried to roll but Taylor's weight
had him pinned.

"Buck'll teach him!"

"You're damned right!"

Raider brought up his left hand, grabbing Taylor by the
throat. He squeezed until the blond man's eyes bugged out.
Taylor pushed his injured hand in the big man's face, trying to
persuade him to let go. Raider opened his mouth and bit into
thick bandage.

When Taylor screamed, the miners leaned in, as if they had
the notion to help. But Raider had already freed himself from
Taylor's weight. As Taylor fell off him, he rolled to the side,
trying to get to his feet. One of the spectators saw fit to kick
him in the ribs.

"No!" Ransom cried. "Let them fight it out between themselves."

Taylor staggered to his feet, taking his bearings.

Raider managed to prop himself on one arm just as his
adversary rushed him again. Taylor intended to apply the toe
of his boot to Raider's tender ribs. He saw the boot coming.
Only he had a big surprise for the blond man.

When Taylor kicked, Raider lifted his left arm, swinging it
behind the man's leg. As he fell to the ground his weight
caught Taylor off balance, and he managed to take the blond
man with him. Raider rolled again, trying to get away from
Taylor long enough to regain his balance.

"Don't let him get away, Buck!"

"Kill the son of a bitch!"

Raider came up on his knees. He put his left hand down
and raised his body until he was standing again. Buck Taylor
had also gotten to his feet.

"Now you're gonna get it, Pinkerton. I'm tired of playing
with you!"

Raider wanted to say something, but he figured it was better to catch his breath. Taylor came on again, only this time he
was slower, more controlled. When he was close enough, he
swung with his left, throwing a round house blow that missed
Raider by a mile.

As the blond man lurched off balance, Raider lifted a kick
that caught him squarely in the groin. Taylor grunted and im-

mediately fell to his knees. Raider didn't wait for him to get up. He kicked again, driving the flat sole of his boot into the man's ugly face. Taylor fell backward with blood gushing from his nose.

Raider kept on using his legs, popping hard kicks into Taylor's ribs and chest. When he saw that the blond man was not going to let up, he backed away, looking down at him. He asked if Taylor had had enough. The blond man only groaned, wrestling with himself on the ground.

"Get up, Buck!"

"Don't quit now, Buck!"

Raider glanced over at Ransom, who was frowning at his fallen champion. "Looks like it's over, Ransom."

Ransom's eyes lifted, glaring in the torchlight. "It ain't over. Get up, Taylor, you sack of shit. You hear me?"

The miners echoed their employer's command. They couldn't believe that Raider had bested their man. The circle seemed to get even tighter around the tall Pinkerton.

Raider scowled at Ransom. "Your boy is down, Levon. It's over. What say we end it right here an' I just ride out?"

Ransom's hateful eyes lifted to Raider. "It ain't over, Pinkerton."

"Look here, Ransom, you set the rules for the fight. Hell, your man even used both hands."

The miners rallied around their boss. Ransom gestured toward his strong man. Two of the miners picked up Taylor and started to drag him toward the cabin at the crest of the hill.

Raider didn't like the look of it. Nobody moved to untie his arm. He began to wriggle, trying to free his right hand.

Ransom pointed at him. "Get the Pinkerton. Get him now!"

The circle closed in as Raider tried to get his hand free. He swung wildly with his left, catching two or three of the miners with useless blows. There were just too many of them pounding on him. He went down in a hail of fists only to be met by as many boots when he hit the ground. Just before he lost consciousness, he wondered if they were going to beat him to death.

When he woke up some time later, he almost wished they had.

•　•　•

Raider opened his black eyes, peering up at a familiar face. He knew the man but he was not sure he could remember the name. He tried to sit up but the pain in his body overcame him.

"Easy there."

The man had red hair and an orange mustache. Where the hell had Raider seen him before? And where the hell was he now?

He tried to speak, but the only word that would come out was, "Who?"

The man squinted at him, frowning. "Hell, Raider, I know you been out for a couple of days, but you mean to say you don't remember your old friend Doc Holliday?"

Raider's head hurt but he managed to make himself remember. It came back slowly to him. At least the part about Tombstone and the fact that he was looking for a killer. The rest was fuzzy.

"Where?" he asked.

Doc Holliday touched a wet cloth to his forehead. "Outside of town," he replied. "At the whorehouse. You remember, the Mexican place. We were out here before."

Raider nodded, although that part was still fuzzy as well.

Holliday lifted a whiskey bottle to Raider's lips. "Here, try this. It might take off some of the rough edges."

The whiskey burned his lips and throat as it went down. Holliday gave him a couple of sips from the bottle and then offered him something from a small brown vial. Raider took the potion, which made the pain ease off some more. He remembered seeing the vial before, but where he could not say.

"Yeah, the women took you for dead when you were dumped on their doorstep," Holliday went on. "But you were still breathing, so they found a bed for you."

Raider tried to sit up again. The pain was still there. It was a little easier to talk, however. "Who brought me here?"

"I suppose it was Doc Bascomb," Holliday replied. "The girls said an old man in a buggy dropped you off."

The big man felt the rush of memory coming back to him. He recalled riding to both mines west of Tombstone. He remembered facing Buck Taylor with his hand tied behind his back. Flashes of riding in a buckboard, being dumped near a running creek. Doc Bascomb must have doubled back to look for him. Had the old boy been watching from the trees when Ransom's men kicked Raider's ass?

Holliday took a pull from the bottle, leaning back in a wooden chair. "Yeah, I came out two days ago to have a little fun. Seems I'm always running away from this one gal name of Katie Elder. Ever hear of her?"

Raider shook his head.

"Just as well," Holliday replied.

He took a swallow from the same brown vial that Raider had sipped from. What was it the doctor had said about the soothing liquid? Some kind of opium?

"Yeah, women can be a lot of trouble," Holliday went on. "Tie you down. Make you do things you don't want to do."

Raider figured Holliday was right, but he didn't dwell on the words that issued from the gambler's mouth. He was thinking about Levon Ransom, about the way the miner had ordered his men to attack him. Ransom had to be hiding something, otherwise he wouldn't have wanted Raider out of the way. Still, he had chosen not to kill the big Pinkerton. Maybe he figured a good beating was enough to discourage the investigation.

Holliday leaned toward Raider a little. "Pinkerton, who did this to you? Who beat you to a pulp?"

"Ransom."

The gambler laughed. "That little pissant?"

Raider asked for water. After he had wet his throat, he tried to talk again. He told Holliday everything he could remember.

The gambler shook his head, leaning back again. "Damn. I knew Ransom wasn't one to be trifled with. I guess this proves it."

"He's got a lid on this thing," Raider offered. "I'm pretty sure he knows why those men were killed. Probably had Taylor kill them."

Holliday whistled. "Whew, that's a big deal, Raider. Ransom has some power in this territory. Somebody said he knows the territorial governor."

"I don't give a shit if he knows God almighty," the big man replied. "I aim t' get t' the bottom o' this."

He tried to sit up, but the pain came back. Holliday urged him to stay still. He offered Raider more whiskey and another pull from the brown vial. Raider drank the hooch but refused the opium.

"Doc Bascomb said that stuff gets you in trouble," Raider offered.

Holliday shrugged. "Keeps me from coughing."

Raider closed his eyes, taking inventory of his body. His arms and legs had not been broken. Face intact, probably because he had covered up while the miners were kicking him. Most of the damage had been done to his ribs and back.

Holliday put the whiskey bottle in Raider's hand. "Sleep it off, pilgrim. You're too damned tough. They'll never kill you."

Raider wasn't sure about that, but he fell asleep before he could think on it anymore.

When the woman started screaming, Raider thought he was having a bad dream. He waited for her to stop, but she kept on, yowling like a banshee. His eyes opened to the first light of day. He was still in the cantina. He had slept through the night.

"Help. Please!"

Raider sat up, finding that he could now move a little better. Slowly he came off the bed, touching his feet to the cool floor. The woman screamed again and another woman joined her, yelling in Spanish. Raider started through the morning shadows, following the sounds of their voices.

He found both of them bending over Doc Holliday. The dentist looked dead. His face was white and his eyes were rolled back in his head. Raider saw the brown vial lying next to him. The damned gambler had taken too much of Doc Bascomb's medicine.

Raider looked at the women. "Okay, get him up."

They stared wide-eyed at him.

"I mean it," he insisted. "Help me get him outside."

"Is he dead, señor?"

Raider touched Holliday's skin. "He's still warm, but he won't be for long if we don't get him outta here."

The three of them dragged Holliday outside to the horse trough. Raider managed to roll the gambler into the cold water. At first there was no response, but then Holliday stirred and rolled his head back.

"Don't bother me now, Katie," he muttered.

Raider told one of the women to slap him hard in the face. They both complied, hitting him several times. Holliday's eyes opened.

"Why're you hitting me?"

Raider shook his head, exhaling. "Well, he's alive. Has he got a horse 'round here?"

One of the women pointed to a shed out back. At Raider's insistence, she went to get the mount. When she led the horse to the water trough, Raider grabbed the gambler and lifted him onto the animal's bare back.

"What the hell're you doing?" Holliday said as he grabbed the horse's mane.

"Savin' your fool neck," Raider replied.

He told the women to make sure Holliday rode the animal until he was able to walk again. Then he slapped the horse on the rump and it started walking in the direction of the shed. The women followed, laughing at the spectacle.

Raider went back into the cantina where the proprietor met him. The Mexican man asked if Raider was hungry. To his surprise, the big man found his stomach was ready for food. He ate a big plate of beans and then went back to bed for a while. About noon, he was startled by someone shaking him from his nap.

"Damn you, Pinkerton!" said Doc Holliday.

Raider opened his eyes to a pitiful sight. Holliday, who was as white as snow, stood shaking over his bed. His lips were blue and his hair looked like straw grass. At least he was still alive.

"Are you the one who put me on that horse?" Holliday cried.

Raider had to laugh. "It was the only way t' save your neck, Holliday."

"I oughta—"

"You oughta get some sleep," Raider offered. "You look like hell."

They probably would have bantered back and forth, but the proprietor of the cantina came rushing in on them. "Señores, someone is coming!"

Raider got out of bed, wishing that his gun had not been taken by Levon Ransom. With Holliday dogging his steps, he went to the front window of the cantina. When he peered out, he saw Wyatt Earp tying his horse to the hitching post. The marshal wore his usual grim face.

They went out to meet Earp, who stopped dead when he saw them.

"Figured I might find you here," the marshal said.

Raider shrugged. "It's a long story, Earp. I—"

The marshal raised his hand. "Save it. There's been trouble out at the Ransom mines. They sent a man in to get me. I thought it was you at first, Raider, but the man said you weren't there."

"Another killin'?" Raider asked.

Earp nodded. "That man name of Buck Taylor. Died this mornin'."

Raider could not believe what he had heard. He figured to tell Earp about his fight with Taylor on the way out to the mines. He was still hurting, but nothing was going to keep him away. Not even if it meant that he would have to borrow a horse and a gun from Doc Holliday.

CHAPTER SEVENTEEN

By late afternoon, Raider and Earp reined up at the sign marking the direction to the Ransom Ore Mines. Raider shifted in the saddle, wishing Doc Holliday kept a canteen on his mount. Earp took a canteen from his own saddle and offered it to the big man from Arkansas. Raider grimaced as the warm water went down. Sweat poured off his forehead, streaming down his rugged face.

Earp eyed the tall Pinkerton as he took back the water bottle. "You look to be in a sorry state, Raider. What the devil happened to you?"

"Taylor," he replied. "We had a fight an' I won. Only Ransom d'cided t' put his men on me. 'Bout twenty-five of 'em."

"You're lucky they didn't kill you."

Raider felt the hitch in his ribs. "Yeah, lucky."

He turned the horse to the north.

"Pinkerton."

"Yeah, Marshal?"

Earp frowned at him. "You say you was scrappin' with Taylor."

"Yeah. He had a bandage on his hand, where I thought mebbe I shot him in the alley. So Ransom tied a hand b'hind my back."

"And Taylor was the one who gave you the whippin'?"

Raider exhaled, wishing the pain in his body would go away. "Taylor didn't whip me. It was Ransom's men."

"Taylor's dead," Earp offered.

Raider squinted at the lawman. "Go on an' say what's on your mind, Earp."

"Some might say you killed him."

"Some might."

He spurred Doc Holliday's mount, heading for the mines. Earp fell in behind him. They rode hard to the north until they saw the road leading up to Ransom's digs.

Raider slowed when he reached the base of the road. Earp came up beside him. They both searched the trees, looking for sentries.

"I left my sorrel in these trees a few nights ago," Raider said. "I wonder if Ransom's men found her?"

"Maybe we oughta go straight in before we worry about your mount."

Raider agreed that was the thing to do. He started slowly up the incline, his hand hovering around the .38 Diamondback that Holliday had loaned him. Funny, he thought, his old partner and Holliday sharing the same monicker and carrying the same kind of gun. He'd think about it later, after he had unraveled some of the unlikely happenings at Ransom Ore.

"He had four sentries on duty the last time I was here," he told Earp.

The marshal lifted his Buntline from the holster, spinning the cylinder. He held the Buntline in hand, watching the trail as they drew closer to the camp. Raider realized he had never seen the marshal shoot before. He hoped Earp knew how to use the long-barreled pistol. It would sure as hell come in handy to have another gun along.

"You know, Earp, if you'd come out with me the first time, I wouldn't've had my butt kicked by Ransom's men."

Earp pulled at the brim of his Stetson. "Maybe. Maybe not. They might have kicked mine too."

"I wanna know somethin', Marshal. Do you have any jurisdiction out here, or are we blowin' smoke?"

Earp drew a long breath. "I got jurisdiction here. This is part of my territory. I just always left it alone because it never had much to do with Tombstone."

"Well, Marshal, it's 'bout time you started doin' your duty."

They urged the horses closer to the camp.

Raider expected the sentries to be posted on top of the buildings, but the rooftops were empty. He also thought the miners would be at work on the slopes above, but instead, they were milling about in their quarters. Some of them seemed to be packing their belongings.

Several men watched Raider and the marshal as they rode toward the main lodge where Ransom stayed. Raider cast dirty looks at them, like he figured to settle the score for the beating he'd suffered. The miners weren't so brave in broad daylight, facing two armed men. Mobs had a lot more guts than single men. Most men would back off if they had to look you in the eye.

Earp seemed to read the big man's thoughts. "I could arrest them all, run them in for gangin' up on you."

Raider considered it but shook his head. "I ain't the spiteful kind, Marshal. Besides, I'm sure every one o' those chicken-peckers has seen more'n his share o' beatin's. How else could a man gang up on another?"

Earp shook his head in disbelief. "For an arrogant son of a buck, you sure come out with some noble thoughts."

Raider chortled cynically. "Noble, huh? Yeah, I reckon that's me."

As they approached the hitching post, the planked lodge door swung open. A drawn and shaking Levon Ransom approached them. Raider had never seen the little weasel in good light. He looked like something that had been chased out from under a rock.

"Thank God," he said weakly. "Thank God you're here."

Raider swung down, grunting when the ground jolted him. He gritted his teeth, trying to shunt off the urge to draw the Diamondback and pistol-whip the man who had sanctioned his merciless beating. He'd save that pleasure for after Ransom's confession.

"Taylor's dead," Ransom groaned. "Dead."

Earp was hitching his mount to the post. "Calm down, Mr. Ransom."

The miner cast his gaze down the incline, toward the encampment. "They're all leaving me alone," he intoned dolefully. "They're deserting me. Leaving to go to work for Clairborn."

Raider and Earp grabbed Ransom's arms, leading him back toward the lodge.

The miner went on ranting. "Clairborn is behind this, I tell you. He wanted all my men to come to work for him. Just the way he stole Lucius. And then he killed him!"

They dragged him through the house, plopping him in a chair. Ransom immediately reached for a bottle of brandy. He poured a large cupful and knocked it back.

Earp frowned at the miner. "He seems to have lost his senses."

Raider grabbed the brandy bottle. "He's drunk. An' he's smoked his brains out. Look. There must be twenty-five butts from hand-rolls. He's just stewed."

Ransom reached for the brandy bottle, whining like a child. "No, don't take that from me. I need it."

Raider reached back and flung the bottle all the way across the room. Glass shattered on the other wall, leaving a splotch of brandy that soaked into the wood. Earp flinched when the glass exploded.

"My brandy!"

Raider pointed a finger at Ransom. "You're gonna drink coffee, you little pissant."

Ransom put his head in his hands. "My brandy—"

Raider grabbed the front of the miner's coat and pulled him out of the chair. "I oughta whip your ass right now, Ransom. Pay you back for what your men did t' me."

Ransom only whimpered.

Earp's hand rested on the butt of the Buntline. "Raider, you don't have to do this."

The big man dropped Ransom back in the chair. He turned to glare at the marshal. "You hired me t' see t' this thing, Earp. Now, you want me t' do my job or you wanna take over?"

The marshal sighed. "Do your job."

Raider turned to the miner again. "Ransom."

He was reaching for his tobacco pouch.

Raider knocked the pouch away from him. "You can

smoke later. Right now I want you t' point the way t' Taylor's body."

Ransom lowered his head. "Buck. He was a good man. I only hired him a couple of months ago. But you need somebody like that if you're going to have a lot of silver around. Yes, you need somebody like that."

"Where's the body, Ransom?"

The weak face turned upward, scowling at Raider. "You! You killed Buck. You came in here and stirred up my men with stories of killin's. But you're the murderer. The blood is on your hands."

Raider didn't hit him hard. It was just a light slap with the tips of his fingers. The blow caught Ransom on his chin. It didn't even turn his head much, but it did snap him back to the matters at hand.

After he had stopped whimpering, Raider grabbed his collar again. "Now tell me what you did with Taylor."

"Out back," was Ransom's only reply.

Raider turned to Earp. "I'm gonna have a look-see."

"Want me to come with you?"

He shook his head. "Stay with the weasel here. See if you can get some coffee into him. Let him have another cigarette."

Earp nodded. "I want to look at the body too."

"You'll have your chance, Marshal. You'll have your chance."

The body of Buck Taylor had been covered with a canvas tarp. Raider pulled it back, looking down at the white face of the dead man. Blood covered Taylor's chest and neck. His eyes were half-open, rolled back into his head. Blue lips, faded skin.

Raider tore away the blood-soaked shirt, looking at the bare chest. He nodded to himself. A few things started to focus. He touched Taylor's deathly skin. What the hell had happened? He thought he was starting to understand.

He pulled the canvas over Taylor's pallid face and went back into the lodge.

Earp was handing Ransom a steaming cup of coffee. He turned to Raider. "Well?"

Raider pointed with his thumb. "Go have a look." He wanted Earp out of the room when he talked to Ransom.

The marshal hitched up his pants, like he was bracing for the spectacle.

"There's a lotta blood," Raider offered.

Earp tried to swallow. "I've seen bodies before. Blood too."

When he was gone, Raider turned to the miner. "What happened, Ransom? How did Taylor git it?"

The miner took a deep breath. "I sent him out back to get some wood for the stove. I heard a shot. When I went out, he was covered with blood, lying on the ground."

"Did you see who shot him?"

Ransom shook his head.

Earp came back into the room. "He's dead all right."

Raider looked sideways at the marshal. "Did you take a close look at Taylor's chest?"

"I most surely did,"

"Notice anything strange?" Raider asked slyly.

Earp frowned. "What are you talkin' about?"

Raider shrugged. "Nothin'. He's dead all right. Ransom said he heard the shot an' everythin'."

"Does he know who did it?" Earp wondered aloud.

"Says he don't. You don't know, do you, Levon?"

Ransom glared at him. "You had the beef with Taylor," the miner said pointing at Raider. "He whipped you."

"That's bullshit," the big man replied. "I put him on the ground and then you put your men on me. If I got a beef with anyone, it's you, Ransom."

Earp eyed the irate Pinkerton agent. "You were the last one to tangle with Taylor, Raider."

Without hesitation, Raider asked Ransom, "What time was Taylor killed?"

"This morning."

He turned to Earp. "I been in that cathouse for two days, Marshal. I was there t'day when Taylor got it. Ask Holliday or those at the cantina."

Earp exhaled defeatedly. "You're always one step ahead of me."

Raider looked back at Ransom. "No, Levon here is the one who's ahead of all of us."

Earp's brow fretted. "Ransom?"

Raider knelt down beside Ransom's chair. "You know

more'n you told me the other day, Levon. Don't you?"

Ransom only nodded.

"What are you talkin' about?" Earp asked.

"Levon here knew that man we found in the alley," Raider replied. "An' I'm bettin' he knew the other two as well."

Earp turned his gaze on the miner. "What of it, Ransom? Is the Pinkerton here tellin' the truth?"

Ransom nodded again. "I knew them," he said in a weak voice. "They served with me at Andersonville. All three. When they came west, they looked me up and asked for jobs. I put them to work."

Earp wasn't sure he knew what Ransom was talking about. "Andersonville? The Confederate prison?"

Ransom nodded. "We all served there together. I was one of their superior officers. It seems like a thousand years ago. Only now it has come back to haunt me. I know it has."

"What about Taylor?" Earp asked. "Did he serve with you at Andersonville?"

Raider looked sideways at the marshal. "Didn't you hear him say he hired Taylor a few months ago?"

"Oh. I reckon I did hear him say that."

Raider regarded the miner again. "Ransom, what were the names o' those other two men who were killed?"

"One was called Fortune, Jake Fortune. The other one was Beau Jackson. They were from Georgia."

Earp reached into his pocket for a pencil and a scrap of paper. He quickly wrote down the two names. He told Raider he would check his office to see if there were any posters on the dead men. Maybe they were wanted for something that would lend a clue to their deaths by torture.

Raider tipped back his Stetson. "You won't find anythin', but it's still a good idea t' look."

Earp bristled. "You think you know everything."

Raider ignored his temper. "Ransom, who you think killed those boys?"

"I don't know," the miner replied. "I surely don't know."

"Mebbe you did it," the big man offered. "Maybe you had Taylor do it for you and then you killed him."

Ransom's weasel-eyes opened wide. "No! Why would I kill them?"

Raider shrugged. "Who knows? Mebbe they wanted you t'

settle an old debt. But you wouldn't come across with the money. You gave 'em jobs t' get 'em off your back, but it wasn't enough. They demanded more, mebbe a share o' your mine. But you wouldn't give it up. Finally you had t' kill 'em t' get 'em outta the way."

"No! It wasn't like that. I didn't owe them a thing. They were happy to get jobs."

"Then why did McCabe go t' work for Clairborn?"

Ransom blushed. "All right, he did demand things from me. He wanted to be made foreman. But I wouldn't have it. So he quit. But I wouldn't kill him for leaving me."

"You lied to me afore, Ransom. Why?"

"I was scared," the miner replied. "I worried that the other men would leave if they knew two of their crewmen had died. Even when the bodies turned up, they didn't know that the men had once worked for me."

Raider exhaled dejectedly. "An' nobody thought anythin' 'bout it when they disappeared."

"Miners will pick up and go," Ransom said. "It's common."

Raider stood up, scowling at the miner. "You could have come t' Earp an' told him 'bout those two dead men. It mighta saved McCabe. Hell, you might as well've killed him yourself."

Ransom began to whimper.

Earp motioned to Raider. He took the big man aside and spoke in a low voice. "What do you really think about all this?"

Raider sighed deeply. "Well, ever'thin' fits 'cept for one thing. Taylor was wounded on the hand. It coulda been him I shot in that alley. It coulda been somebody else."

"If it was Taylor," the marshal offered, "then Ransom is lyin'. Maybe you were right when you said there was bad blood between Ransom and the men who were killed."

"It kinda looks that way. Shit!"

Earp frowned. "What's wrong?"

"We don't have 'nough evidence t' pin all this on Ransom. Not yet anyway. If we're gonna take him in, we've gotta have somethin' t' show a judge. I can't just testify an' say what I think. Hell, I don't know if I'm right or wrong; not really."

Earp rubbed his chin. "This is all too much for me. I've got to take Ransom into town."

"Mebbe not," Raider offered. "Not if you wanna catch the one who really did all this."

"Come again?"

"You cain't trap a fox if you're watchin' the snare, Wyatt."

"Don't talk in riddles, Pinkerton."

"Just this," the big man said, "you gotta leave the trap alone for a spell an' then come back an' check it."

Earp eyed him suspiciously. "What are you up to?"

"Let's leave. Or at least make it look that way. See what Ransom does after we're gone."

Earp wasn't sure he liked the idea, but it seemed to make sense. After all, what did they have? A bunch of dead bodies and no clue as to who had really killed all those men.

"It still made sense what you said before," the marshal said. "Ransom had a grudge against those three men, something that went back to the war. They wanted a share of his mine or something like that. So Ransom hired Taylor to do away with them. Then he killed Taylor and now he's only actin' like he's crazy with grief and fear."

Raider put his hand on Earp's shoulder. "Yeah, it looks that way. But what does the judge say when we tell him all that? He'll ask for evidence. We don't have enough."

"A jury might find him guilty," Earp offered.

Raider dropped his hand. "Just like a lawman. You don't care 'bout justice, long as somebody swings. What if I'm wrong? What if Taylor didn't kill those men? What if somebody just wants us t' think that?"

"Ransom is the only suspect we got."

"Even you don't wanna hang a innocent man, Earp. Do you?"

The marshal bristled a little, but he saw Raider's point. "So what should we do, Mr. Pinkerton?"

"Leave now."

"That's it?"

Raider nodded. "I'll tell you the rest when we hit the trail. But for now, let's just clear the hell out."

Earp nodded. "I'll go along with this for a while, Raider. But I hope you know what you're doin'."

"I don't," the big man replied, "but then agin, neither d' you."

They turned back toward Ransom, who peered expectantly at them.

"Well, we're gonna go back t' Tombstone," Raider offered.

A frightened expression came over the small man's face. "You can't leave me. Not with a killer on the loose."

Raider smiled a little. "You'll be all right, Ransom. Just get a few o' your men t' sit with you."

"They're all quitting me!" the miner said. "You ran them off with your murder talk."

"Don't blame me," the big man replied. "Blame the one who killed Buck Taylor and the rest o' those men."

Ransom started to shake again. "No. You have to protect me. It's your duty! You can't leave me alone. The killer will get me!"

Raider's eyes narrowed. "Why would he want to kill you, Ransom? What did you do?"

"I don't know! Do you hear me? I don't know!"

Earp gestured toward the back. "You'll have t' bury that body, Ransom. Even though this is in my jurisdiction as marshal, it's out of the Tombstone town line. You can't expect the citizens to pay for his burial."

"I'm too weak," the miner cried. "I haven't handled a shovel in years. I couldn't even lift that body."

Raider pointed a finger at him. "You tell us the truth, Ransom. Otherwise we're gettin' the hell outta here."

Ransom put his hands together, like he was begging. "Please. Please don't leave me alone."

"The truth," Raider insisted.

"I've told you everything I know!"

Raider tipped his hat to the weak-faced man. "Adios, Ransom. We'll be in Tombstone if you d'cide t' come clean."

He started for the front door.

Earp fell in behind him.

Ransom's protests rang in their ears as they left.

Earp stopped at the hitching post, gazing back at the lodge. "He sounds like he's really scared."

Raider swung into the saddle. "We'll find out soon 'nough."

Earp mounted up as well. "What do you have in mind?"

"You'll see," the big man replied. "Let's just get outta here for now. I wanna make it look like we're really gone."

Earp shook his head as they turned their horses away from the lodge. As they passed the barracks where the miners were preparing to leave, the lawman had to wonder what Raider had in mind. He figured to go along with the Pinkerton for a while. But if the big man's ploy went bad, the marshal planned to step in and take over.

"How long are we gonna have to wait here?" asked Wyatt Earp.

They were hunkered in the thin trees below the Ransom property line. Raider's mount was nowhere to be found. He wondered who had taken it. Probably one of the miners who had left Ransom's employment.

Raider kept his eyes turned upward, toward the encampment. It was well past sunset, but no lights were glowing from the camp. All of the miners had gone. Most of them had passed Raider and Earp without ever knowing they were hiding in the trees.

Earp shifted nervously in the brush. "Are you gonna answer me?"

"I ain't sure how long we're gonna have t' wait," the big man replied. "I'll know it when it feels right."

Earp exhaled impatiently. "We should've taken Ransom into custody. It was the right thing to do."

"But not the smart thing. An' we can always grab him later t'night, if things don't work out."

Earp shook his head. "I don't know what you're expectin' to work out. And as far as I can see, neither do you."

Raider shrugged. "Well, you're the lawman. You can go up there an' arrest Ransom. Slap him in jail. Take your chances with a judge an' jury. But what will it hurt t' wait another few hours?"

Earp grimaced. "Hours?"

"If it takes that. Like I said, you gotta leave the trap alone for a spell afore you go back an' check it."

The marshal kept shifting where he sat. "What the devil do you think is gonna happen, anyway?"

"You'll find out."

"You saw somethin', didn't you?" the lawman challenged.

"Mebbe."

"Then why don't you tell me what it is?"

An exasperated breath from the tall man. "I don't know, Earp. I reckon I don't wanna look stupid if I'm wrong. And if I'm right, well, let's just say I don't wanna jinx it."

They sat there for a long while without talking. Earp swatted night bugs away from his face. Somewhere a screech owl broke the darkness with its shrill cry. And on the hill above them, a light glowed to life in the murky confines of Ransom's lodge.

Raider got up and started for the road.

"Hey," Earp called. "Is this it?"

"Time t' move," Raider called over his shoulder. "Let's take it slow."

They stepped cautiously through the shadows, making their way beneath the star-spread sky, stopping at the first set of cabins. Everything was quiet. No one stirring, unlike the night when Raider had taken his licks from the mob of miners.

Slipping past the cabins, they made for the main lodge, sticking to the side of the road. Raider figured to play it sneaky. At least until he heard the screaming. Then he broke into a run, with Earp right behind him.

CHAPTER EIGHTEEN

Raider stopped at the door of the lodge. Earp almost slammed into him. Earp started to say something but Raider waved him off. They both listened until the man screamed again.

Earp reached for the door.

Raider knocked his hand away. "No. I'll go in this way. You slide 'round back, come in from the other door."

Earp frowned. "I don't think—"

"Just do it, Earp. If we come at him from two diff'rent angles, he's not likely t' shoot us both."

That seemed logical to the marshal. With his Buntline in hand, he started for the back door. Raider figured to wait a few seconds and then go in. Draw fire from the man who was in there with Ransom. Maybe Earp could get the drop from the back.

Someone hollered again.

Raider tensed, wondering if he was right about a few things. It was going to become clearer when he burst through the door, but the whole picture wouldn't be apparent for a while. He slid against the door, holding Doc's Diamondback to the night sky. One good shove and then lower the gun into the face of the man who had killed all three of the poor miners.

Another scream from inside the cabin.

Nothing to do but go through with it.

He laid his shoulder to the door and knocked it off the hinges.

"Don't move!" he cried, leveling his gun.

The man hovered over Ransom, who had been tied to the chair. Raider could see that the man wore a blue army coat that was too small for him. He turned to regard the Pinkerton who had kicked down the door.

Raider smiled slightly, a smirk of self-satisfaction that made him realize that he had been at least partly right. "Hello, Taylor. Have a good sleep? How's it feel t' return from the dead?"

Buck Taylor's chest was still covered with blood. He scowled at the big man, emitting a low groan from his throat. Raider moved closer to the resurrected henchman, keeping his finger on the trigger of the Diamondback.

Taylor started backing toward a window.

"That's not a smart move, Buck. Not unless you want me t' open a real hole in your chest."

Taylor froze, his wolfish eyes narrowing. "You think you're so damned smart, Pinkerton."

"Not smart as you, Buck. Usin' Doc Bascomb's medicine t' make it look like you was dead. Did he give it t' you when he came out here t' treat your hand?"

Taylor laughed. "You can't prove anything, Pinkerton."

Raider gestured with the barrel of the revolver. "Where'd you get that coat you have on?"

Taylor frowned.

"Yeah, Buck, I found brass buttons from the sleeve o' that coat. Found 'em close t' where two o' them boys was killed. You wanna tell me 'bout the coat, Taylor?"

"I ain't tellin' you shit!"

Keeping his eye on Taylor, Raider started slowly across the lodge. Ransom rested in his chair with thick ropes holding him in place. The miner had round, red marks on his weak face. His eyes were closed and he seemed to have passed out. Raider squinted at the marks on Ransom's face. It appeared that Taylor had been burning his boss with the hot ends of hand-rolled cigarettes.

Raider gaped at the tall blond man. "What the hell is this? Some sorta trick t' make it look like Ransom is one o' your victims? Or did you just turn on him after you did his dirty work?"

"You don't know a damned thing, Pinkerton."

Raider waved the Diamondback. "I knew enough t' spot your little trick, Taylor. Now I got the drop on you. Who's smarter? You or me?"

"You son of a bitch!"

"I hate t' think what you're a son of, Buck. Now put those hands over your head. I'm gonna take you back t' Tombstone. An' Ransom here is gonna come along for the ride."

Taylor started backing toward the rear door. "You ain't takin' me nowhere, you bastard. I ain't payin' for this."

Raider pointed the Diamondback at the center of Taylor's chest. "If you don't come alive, you'll come dead."

Taylor stopped with his back against the door. "Go on, kill me. Do it if you got the guts."

Raider considered honoring Taylor's request. It would save a lot of trouble in the long run. The price of a trial and a rope could be spared. Still, it meant gunning down a man who did not have a weapon on him. At least a weapon that was in sight.

"Raise those hands, Taylor."

"No!"

The big man from Arkansas let out an impatient sigh. "Taylor, I've 'bout had it with you. Put those hands up now!"

Raider figured he had won when the outlaw started to lift his palms to the ceiling. But then something terrible happened. Wyatt Earp decided to make his untimely entrance and everything got confused in a hurry.

Raider had to wonder why the marshal chose the exact wrong moment to shove open the door. Taylor, who had been leaning against the doorway, went sprawling toward the window. Raider turned his gun to fire a warning shot, but Earp stepped between him and Taylor.

"Earp, you greenhorn bastard!" Raider cried.

Taylor's forward motion carried him toward the window.

He dived headlong through the shattering glass, propelling himself into the dark night. Earp had given him the brief moment that he needed to escape.

Raider rushed toward the window, pushing the marshal out of his way. He stuck his gun through the shattered glass, firing two or three shots into the shadows. As the gunsmoke swirled around in the cool air, he hesitated, listening for sounds of feet as they scuffled off into the night. Instead, he heard the unmistakable thud of hooves as a horse galloped away from the mining camp.

"Who the devil was that?" Earp asked.

Raider grimaced at the lawman. "Buck Taylor!"

"What?"

"You heard me. Buck Taylor. Back from the dead. He was workin' on Ransom here."

Earp looked at the unconscious miner. "Why was Taylor tryin' to hurt Ransom? I thought Ransom was his boss."

Raider started for the door. "So did I."

"Where d' you think your goin'?"

"After Taylor."

Earp frowned. "Wait for me."

Raider turned back, pointing to Ransom. "Stay with him. See if you can get him t' wake up. Mebbe he'll tell you the truth now."

"But—"

But Raider was gone.

The big man from Arkansas ran out the front door, wishing that his mount was not tied below the trees. Taylor had been smart to leave his horse nearby. Maybe he was planning to take off as soon as he finished his boss. That was how it seemed.

He tried to make sense of it as he ran down the incline toward the woods where he had left his horse.

Had Taylor faked his death to get Raider off the case?

And if Ransom had hired Taylor to get rid of the three men from Ransom's past, then why had Taylor turned on him?

Surely a weak man like Ransom would not have crossed his bodyguard.

So why the hell had Taylor been torturing the miner? Burning him with lit cigarettes. That sure as hell fell in line with the other deaths by torture. But it was still missing something, the key that pulled it all together.

Raider found his mount and swung into the saddle. The horse came out of the trees wanting to run. But Raider had to rein up, to figure out which direction to chance. Taylor had come straight down the road, It was the only way out of the camp, especially when a man was leaving in a hurry. Raider reined left and made for the open trail.

He knew Taylor could turn any way he wanted once he cleared the trees. Probably he wouldn't head into Tombstone; not if he figured to steer clear of the law. Too hard to go north, unless he wanted to fight the mountains. South. It had to be. Taylor would head for Mexico. There'd be a hell of a price on his head, after killing three men.

Raider spurred the mount he had borrowed from Doc Holliday. He rode steadily, stopping a few times to strike a match over open ground. He searched for the impressions of another set of hoofprints. But the dirt was too hard for a horse to leave much trace that could be found on a moonless night.

Just keep south, he told himself, at least until he hit the Clairborn mines. Check in with Jack Clairborn. Make sure he was all right.

His stomach started to churn as he rode on. Taylor was on the run. He'd need money and guns. Raider had forced him to leave in a hurry. Of course, Taylor could have been ready to go, saddlebags packed with silver that had come from Ransom's mines.

Would Taylor be greedy? Would he pay a visit to Clairborn and take everything he owned? Best to check in with the old miner who didn't even carry a gun. If Taylor wasn't there, Raider could double back in the morning and pick up his trail.

Warm lights burned in the confines of Jack Clairborn's cabin. It was awfully late for a working man to be awake. No lights in the miners' tents. Maybe Clairborn stayed up late to work on his books.

Raider dismounted just below the cabin, tying the horse where he would be able to find it if he had to run again.

With his gun in hand, he started slowly for Clairborn's cabin. Raider stayed in the shadows until he was beside the cabin door. He listened for any telltale sounds. A low wind made the cabin creak. Something rushed to his left. Spinning with the Diamondback, he lowered the barrel at a dark shape that ran by. A loose horse. Had Taylor lost his mount?

There was noise inside the cabin.

Taylor's voice was loud. "You old bastard, where do you keep the silver? Answer me! I'll kill you if you don't tell me!"

Raider crashed through the door. "You ain't killin' nobody, Taylor. Now put your hands—"

The blond man was quick, even with a wounded hand. He had Jack Clairborn by the chin, pulling his head back. A knife blade rested across the old man's Adam's apple.

"One stroke and he'd dead," Taylor said, grinning.

Raider held his gun steady. "Let him go."

Taylor pulled the old man closer to him, using Clairborn's body as a shield. "You won't pull the trigger, Pinkerton. You can't shoot me without shooting him."

Jack Clairborn gaped at the big man. "Don't let him do this to you, Pinkerton. Don't worry about me. Just kill him."

Taylor started to drag Clairborn to the back of the cabin.

Raider stepped after them, waiting for a shot. "If you hurt him, Taylor, I'll put a bullet 'tween your eyes."

"Just don't fire that hogleg and we'll all get outta this alive," Taylor offered. "Steady. Wouldn't want my hand to slip and take this old fool's head off."

"Kill him, Pinkerton!" old Clairborn cried. "Don't let him push us around like this."

"Hush up, Jack," Raider replied. "Just stay still an'—"

Taylor bumped the back door. He kicked back, knocking it open. Then he dropped Clairborn and fled again into the night.

"Should've killed him," Clairborn said, rubbing his neck.

Raider stepped out the back door and looked into shadows. "Damn."

Taylor was too quick.

"That does it," the big man said to himself. "Next time I get the drop on him, I'll have t' kill him."

CHAPTER NINETEEN

Jack Clairborn stood up, brushing himself off. "He won't get away," the miner said. "And you'll get your chance to kill the bastard."

Raider turned back to the miner. "Thought you was a peace-lovin' man, Clairborn. Changed your mind, did you?"

Clairborn frowned. "I can't be tolerable of them that do me wrong. Not the likes of that ape."

"I reckon it's different when it's personal-like."

Clairborn gestured to the night. "Just go after him. I'll stir things up in a hurry. He won't get away."

Raider wondered what Clairborn meant as he stepped into the shadows. Then he heard the clang of a dinner bell. Clairborn was waking his miners, which could be bad or good, depending on how it was handled.

He stopped, taking a deep breath. Taylor would have to be found quickly, otherwise he would surely get away. The miners could come in handy, but Raider had to talk to them first. Get things straight and then spread out, drive Taylor right into a trap.

But it had to be done right.

• • •

The miners rallied quickly with their torches overhead, like men who had often heard the call of disaster and calamity in the middle of the night. They gathered in front of the cabin, gaping at Raider and Clairborn. Some of them carried pistols and rifles. Raider figured eighteen or twenty in all.

He raised his hands into the torchlight. "Now listen up, boys. There's a tall blond man runnin' 'round here. We gotta catch him. You two, head for the stables. Ten of you line up on the road, all the way to the end of the trail."

They obeyed as if they were soldiers.

"You three with the guns, stay here with Clairborn. The rest o' you men with the guns, go in diff'rent directions. Don't shoot anybody 'less they start shootin' at you."

Three men came beside Clairborn and the others spread out into the night.

Two men had been left with nothing to do.

"Can you boys ride?" Raider asked.

They both nodded.

"Then one o' you ride my mount. It's tied below, on the left. I think I tied it on a pump."

The man said he would have no trouble finding it.

"What you want me to do?" the last man asked.

"There's a horse runnin' loose 'round here," Raider replied. "See if you can find it an' then holler when you do."

"Yes, sir."

Raider turned back to Clairborn. "I shoulda sent a couple of 'em up t' the mines."

"Me and these three will go," Clairborn offered.

Raider nodded. "Just be careful, Jack. He's faster'n a copperhead who ain't et in a month o' Sundays."

"An eye for an eye," Clairborn replied. "Come on, gents. Let's have a look up there, just like the Pinkerton said."

Raider touched the butt of his gun. He realized he had to reload. Best to fill all six chambers. Maybe, if the search went well, he'd get a shot at Taylor by morning.

The tall, blond man ran them a good chase into the night. He was fast and sneaky. A bad combination if you were trying to find somebody in the dark. Still, he wasn't able to get through them, at least not right away.

The first scuffle came almost immediately, down by the stable. Raider had been right to send two men near the horses. Taylor came at them with his knife in hand, but he was unable to hit either one of them.

By the time Raider got there, the commotion had already ended. Taylor was gone again in the shadows, as elusive as a Mescalero Apache. Raider told the two men to stay at the stable in case Taylor returned.

He hadn't taken two steps when the shooting started. Three explosions, two pistols and one rifle. The muzzle flashes illumined the dark road where the line of men was standing.

Raider hollered down the road. "Turn him back. Spread out that way an' don't shoot anythin'!"

The men obeyed, forming a barrier against the fleeing outlaw.

"There he is," somebody cried.

Two more shots.

"Damn it!" Raider cried. "I told you not t' shoot."

"But I saw him!"

Raider listened, wondering if he heard Taylor moving back toward the stable. Or was that the sound of the miners? He told them to stop, to be still. They came to a halt, listening with him.

"Taylor!" he cried into the darkness. "Give it up!"

"There he is!" cried the men from the stable.

Raider wheeled and retraced his steps.

One of the men cried out. When Raider came on them, they seemed to be wrestling with someone. He lowered the bore of the Diamondback, pressing it against the intruder's back.

"Don't move or I'll open you up!"

The two miners scuffled out from under the dark shape.

"He came out of nowhere!"

"Jumped right on us!"

Raider rolled the dead weight over. "You boys were tricked."

They gaped at the dark figure. "What the hell?"

"Got a garden nearabouts?" Raider asked.

They both said there was a corn patch below camp.

Raider held up a scarecrow. "Taylor put his coat on this straw man. He used it t' git by you."

"He didn't get a horse, though."

"No, we didn't let him get a horse!"

Raider told them to stay with the remuda, to hang on to the dummy and the blue army coat. It would serve as evidence for the trial. If there was a trial. It seemed that catching Taylor alive was less and less a possibility. Raider had a feeling he was going to have to put a bullet in the blond man to get him to sit still.

"Hey, Pinkerton. Up here!"

Raider ran toward the sound of the man's voice. He had been following tracks that led in the direction of the mines. Taylor was making for the mountains. Did he really think that was his best chance for escape?

"Pinkerton!"

Raider heard the horse snorting. The shapes moved in front of him. He thumbed back the hammer of the Colt.

"No, Pinkerton! It's me! You sent me to look for the mount!"

Raider uncocked the gun. "Shouldn't sneak up on a man like that."

"Sorry."

Raider took the horse's reins. Was it the same one he had seen running loose before? The animal shook its head.

"Did you see Taylor?" Raider asked.

"I ain't sure. I thought I heard somethin' runnin' away, but when I went to look, nothin' was there."

The big man stared toward the mountains, which loomed against the night sky. As dark as it was, the peaks still stood out against the stars. Maybe the mountains were Taylor's best chance, if he could hide long enough or get to the other side of the range.

"Did it sound like a man on foot?" Raider asked.

"I ain't sure. But I think that Taylor could be on a mule."

Raider's head snapped back. "What makes you say that?"

"Well, ol' Squeaky Henderson keeps his mule tied up behind the woodshed, seein's how he don't like the mule to stay with the other horses. And when I looked behind the woodshed, right before I caught this animal, Squeaky's mule wasn't there."

"Damn."

Raider swung into the saddle. Would Taylor still head into the mountains now that he was riding? Raider urged the horse toward the dark peaks, moving hard until he saw the flickering torches in the distance.

Raider saw Clairborn and his three men as they made their way from the mines. They were leading a mule down the path. Clairborn waved when he saw Raider approaching.

"Found this critter back there," the miner offered. "Squeaky Henderson must not've tied him up too good."

"It was Taylor," the big man replied. "He got 'round you."

One of the men leaned in. "Now hold on, Pinkerton. We just walked down that narrow trail. Ain't no way he could have got around us."

Raider came out of the saddle. "Take my word for it, he got around you. Probably hid in a crack and came out b'hind you."

Clairborn shook his head. "Why the hell is he goin' up there?"

Raider stared at the hills above him. "He thinks he can get away. Is this the only trail up?

"Well, yeah," Clairborn replied. "At least right here. But there is another trail that way."

He pointed to the southwest.

"Does Taylor know this country?"

Clairborn shrugged. "How should I know?"

Raider nodded. "That was a stupid question. I thought mebbe you knew him."

"I know plenty after this night."

Raider handed him the reins of Taylor's mount. "You take these boys an' go wait at the end o' that other trail. If Taylor comes down, shoot the hell outta him. Don't talk t' him, don't give him another chance t' git away. Just fill the son of a bitch full o' lead."

Clairborn eyed the tall Pinkerton. "Are you goin' up after him?"

Raider grabbed one of the torches. "I sure as hell am. If I ain't back by mornin', go find Marshal Earp. He'll either be at Ransom's or in Tombstone. You got that?"

Clairborn nodded.

Raider took a deep breath and started up the trail.

All signs of Taylor led upward, toward the crest of the ridge.

Raider had used the torch for a while, just to make sure he was on the right path. He threw the torch away when he found the broken heel from one of Taylor's boots. A few yards up the trail, he found the second heel. Taylor had removed the heel himself so his boots would be even.

Raider paused on the path, trying to remember the layout of Clairborn's dig. He had seen the spread from below and he was pretty sure that Taylor was climbing toward the highest of Clairborn's mineshafts. He had to smile. There was no place to go after Taylor reached the mine. Only a sheer cliff and rocks above the adit.

With his gun leading the way, Raider eased toward the mine, figuring that Taylor had gone inside. When he reached the mouth of the shaft, he peered into the deep recess. Too dark to walk into. Maybe there was a lamp somewhere near the entrance.

He found a miner's lantern with a couple of sulphur matches wedged between the glass and frame. After the orange flame glowed to life, he still did not want to enter the mine. So he waited, watching the eastern sky as the sun began to rise above the horizon.

When the light poured over the rocks above him, he stood up, figuring that he had to go into the mine to find Taylor. It was then that he heard the rocks falling from the higher slopes. He looked up to see the man who seemed to be coming out of the sky. It was Buck Taylor and he had a knife clutched in his left hand.

CHAPTER TWENTY

Raider lifted the Diamondback, firing one shot before Taylor landed squarely on him. He fell back against the ground, trying to hang on to his gun. The air left his lungs and his chest burned. The first shot had missed. Taylor swung the knife, barely missing Raider's forehead.

The big man felt the weight on top of him. He reached for the left wrist of his assailant, wishing the air would come back inside him. If he didn't suck wind pretty soon, Taylor's knife would find its mark.

"You son of a bitch!" He said it all in one rushing oath.

Taylor lifted the knife to the heavens.

Raider caught his wrist as the blade came down.

Taylor immediately popped him in the face with his bad hand. Raider felt the sweat as it ran down his face. He tried to lift the Diamondback but Taylor had him pinned. The outlaw drove his knee into Raider's groin, causing the big man to grunt and go weak.

Raider tried to hang on to Taylor's wrist, but he felt the blond man pull away. If only he could free his gun. His head was spinning. He saw Taylor lift the blade, which caught the first rays of morning light.

"Good-bye, Pinkerton. Let the devil buy you a drink in Hell!"

Raider's gun was pinned against the rocks. He struggled to get it out. The knife dropped toward him. It seemed to be coming slowly, as if Taylor was savoring each moment of Raider's helplessness.

A gun exploded, but it didn't belong to Raider.

Taylor screamed, dropping the knife. He pulled his left hand close to his body, rolling off Raider to squirm into the entrance of the mine.

"The next one will be in your gut," came the voice from the trail.

Raider tried to sit up. "Who the hell is that?"

Wyatt Earp climbed toward the mine. "It's me, Raider. I followed you out here. Clairborn said you chased Taylor into the hills."

Raider's eyes focused on the somber face of the lawman. Earp held the smoking Buntline in his hand. Raider figured the marshal knew how to use a pistol after all.

Taylor started to move, like he wanted to scramble to his feet.

Earp swung the barrel of the Buntline, catching Taylor near the temple of the right side of his head.

The outlaw fell back on the ground, wrestling with his pain.

Earp shook his head. "I'd kill him if I didn't have a bunch of questions I want to ask him." He looked back at Raider. "You gonna make it, Pinkerton?"

Raider nodded, although it hurt his head to acknowledge the marshal. "Give me a hand, Earp. That bastard got me in the balls."

Earp helped him stagger to his feet.

Taylor groaned again, prompting the marshal to kick him in the ribs.

"Don't kill him, Wyatt," Raider said. "Not yet."

Earp glared at him. "You're lucky I came after you, Pinkerton. Why, if Ransom hadn't died when he did—"

Raider's eyes narrowed. He suddenly forgot about the pain. Something else clicked in.

"Ransom died?"

Earp snapped his fingers. "Just that quick. Slumped over in his chair. I reckon his heart just gave out."

Raider gritted his teeth. "You been had, Wyatt. There's a good chance Ransom ain't really dead."

The marshal frowned. "Come again?"

Raider pointed to Taylor, who was trying to get up again. "That one used some o' Doc Bascomb's medicine t' make hisself look dead. It's the same stuff Holliday drinks t' stop his coughin'. You followin' me?"

"I'm not sure."

"Ransom," the big man replied. "He made it look like Taylor was tryin' t' kill him. Then when I take off after Taylor, he drinks this medicine and he appears t' die. You leave an' now he's prob'ly halfway t' Phoenix."

Earp's face turned bright red. "Damn him." He turned and kicked Taylor again. "Damn both of them."

Raider started down the trail. "Take care o' Taylor," he called over his shoulder. "I'll git back t' Ransom's soon's I can. Maybe I can catch him tryin' t' git away."

Earp called something back in protest, but Raider didn't really hear it. He hurried to get off the mountain. When he found Earp's horse below, he mounted it and rode hard back to the north.

Raider dismounted, tying the horse to the post in front of Ransom's cabin. He drew his gun and strode toward the splintered door. Stepping over the wreckage, he peered into the morning shadows. A lump rested in Levon Ransom's chair.

"Git up," Raider said. "Come on, the game's over."

But Ransom didn't move.

Raider went over and touched the body. It fell out of the chair, slumping to the floor. The big man half-expected Ransom to open his eyes and pull a weapon on him. But Ransom just lay there.

Raider put his fingers against the man's neck. No pulse. Ransom's skin was cold and blue. He was stone dead.

Raider stood up, wondering if it was really over. Somehow

none of it seemed right, but then he would have to put it together later so it would all make sense. Best for now to get Ransom's body on a horse and take it into Tombstone. Another resident for Boot Hill.

He found himself wishing that Ransom hadn't died. Raider had wanted to hear the story firsthand from the man who had arranged the whole thing. At least that was how it looked. Only the last trick had failed. The final dose of Doc Bascomb's elixir had been fatal.

Raider found another horse and loaded Ransom for his last ride.

He met Wyatt Earp on the trail back to Tombstone. The marshal had hog-tied Buck Taylor and put him on the bed of a buckboard wagon borrowed from Jack Clairborn. Taylor had been gagged as well.

They exchanged glances at their prisoners.

"Got him trussed up pretty good, don't you, Marshal?" Raider grinned like a coyote over a fresh carcass. "Gagged him too."

"He wouldn't shut up." Earp pointed to Levon Ransom. "Yours ain't alive."

"No, he's just like you said. I got most of it figgered, but I'd still like t' study on it a spell."

Earp agreed. He wanted to think about it as well. Everything had been so confused. It would take both of them to figure out the entire plan. And even then they'd have a few doubts.

Wyatt Earp sat wearily at his desk, saying it all one more time so he could have it straight for himself. Raider was pretty tired, too. He sure as hell didn't feel like hearing it all again. He had originally explained it to the marshal, so he knew it backward and forward.

"So Ransom was responsible for those three men who were killed," the marshal said.

Raider nodded. "That's it, Wyatt."

The marshal gestured toward the jail cell where Buck Taylor lay sleeping. "Ransom hired Taylor to do his dirty work. Then they both tried to fool us by pretendin' they were dead."

"You ever see Doc Holliday when he's had too much?" Raider offered.

Earp had to admit it made sense, as farfetched as it seemed

on the surface. "I never would have seen it that way."

"Ransom just took a little too much," Raider said. "His heart couldn't take it. He wasn't young like Taylor."

Earp nodded appreciatively. "You saw it clear all along."

"Not all along," the big man replied. "But when I saw the body of Buck Taylor, I didn't notice no bullet hole on his bloody chest. That's when I remembered the way Doc Holliday looked the other day at the cantina. Taylor's face and lips had the same color. And Doc Bascomb had been out t' treat Taylor's hand. That's when he gave him the pain-killer."

Earp sighed, wiping his eyes. "I wish we could have talked to Ransom. He could have told us why he had those men killed."

Raider shrugged, hoping he could escape to a bottle of whiskey and a warm bed. "Who knows why he had Taylor kill 'em? They all went through the war t'gether. Times like that, men make promises that they may not wanna keep later. Those three showed up here, makin' demands on Ransom. Maybe they saved his ass an' he promised t' make 'em all rich some day. Only Ransom don't wanna part with it now that he's rich. So he gives 'em jobs an' then picks 'em off one at a time."

Earp looked puzzled. "But why were they killed in such a horrible way? Tortured like that?"

"Taylor is a mean, loco son of a bitch," the big man replied. "He enjoyed ever' bit of it."

"Then he's gonna hang," Earp said. "As soon as the judge gets here and finds him guilty."

"Mebbe Taylor can tell us why Ransom wanted those three dead. I'm bettin' it has somethin' t' do with Andersonville prison. That's where they all served together."

Earp exhaled defeatedly. "Never heard too much good about that place. I reckon it could have driven men to—"

Somebody knocked on the front door of the Marshal's office. Earp told the visitor to enter. Doc Bascomb came in with his black bag. He nodded to Raider and the marshal.

"Hear you boys have had some commotion," Bascomb said.

Raider winked at the old boy. "Yeah, Wyatt here done all the work. I just tagged along."

Earp ignored Raider's comment. "Thanks' for comin',

Doc. I want you to have a look at somebody for me."

Bascomb gestured toward the jail cell. "I know what you want. It's all over town. You got that Buck Taylor locked up here. He's the one who killed a bunch of men. Rumor has it that he also killed his old boss, Levon Ransom?"

Earp frowned at the physician. "Can you settle somethin' for us, Doc?"

"I'll try, gentlemen."

Raider asked the question. "Just this, Doc. When you were up at the mine fixin' Taylor's hand, did you give him a bottle o' that opium stuff you gave t' Holliday?"

"Gave him two bottles," the doctor replied. "He was a big man and he needed twice the dosage."

Raider snapped his fingers at the marshal. "I told you, Earp. Just like I said. An' it fits!"

Earp nodded his concession to Raider's theory.

Bascomb's brow fretted. "I'm afraid you've lost me, gentlemen. Mind if you let me in on the joke? Or am I in some kind of trouble?"

Raider chortled at the old man. "Naw, just go on in there an' bandage up Taylor's other hand. There's a deputy in there t' guard you."

Bascomb started for the cell room.

Earp stopped him. "Doc Bascomb, you don't carry any firearms, do you?"

"Never have cared much for guns," the doctor replied. "Can't say as I approve of them."

Earp waved him through.

Raider got up out of his chair.

"Where you going?" the marshal asked.

"T' git some food an' some sleep," the big man replied. "If it's all right with you."

"I want you to go over it again with me," Earp said. "See if we left anything out."

Raider groaned, slumping back into the chair. Earp was going to bore him to death. The marshal started off again, at least until the shooting started. Then the office was full of smoke and confusion. And no man could have anticipated what happened next.

CHAPTER TWENTY-ONE

Raider and Earp filled the doorway of the cellroom. The deputy was lying on the floor with blood oozing from his back. Doc Bascomb stood over the deputy, staring wide-eyed at the wound.

Buck Taylor had his back to the wall of the cell. He held a rifle in his bandaged hands. Raider had to wonder how the hell he had gotten the Winchester away from Earp's deputy.

"Back off!" Taylor said. "I'm walkin' out of here, Marshal, and you're not gonna stop me. I don't care if I have to kill all of you."

Earp let out a deep breath. "You aren't goin' anywhere, Taylor. Now put down the rifle before I have to shoot you."

Taylor spat at them. "Back off. I mean it!"

Raider flinched when Earp drew his Buntline. "Are you loco, Earp?"

The marshal started slowly toward Taylor. "You won't make it out of here," he told the outlaw. "I got men in the street. They'll see you and cut you down."

"Better'n hangin' by a rope," Taylor replied. "And I can take a few of them with me. At least have a fightin' chance."

Earp stopped in the open doorway of the cell. "Give it up, Taylor. Take your punishment like a man. You can pay the hangman for a good knot."

Raider held his breath, wondering why the hell Earp had suddenly become so brave. Did he really think Taylor was going to give up the rifle? The big man's hand rested on the handle of his gun. If Taylor plugged the marshal, then Raider was going to avenge Earp's death right away.

Earp held out his hand. "The rifle, Taylor. Otherwise I have to put one between your eyes."

Taylor levered the Winchester. "So long, Marshal. I wish I could say that it's been good to know you."

Raider's pistol was halfway out of the holster when Taylor pulled the trigger of the Winchester. He flinched as the hammer clicked harmlessly against the firing pin. Taylor's face slacked into an expression of dismay.

"Give me the rifle," Earp demanded.

Taylor levered the weapon and pulled the trigger again. Nothing. His body began to tremble.

Raider eased his Colt back into the holster. "Well I'll be damned."

"Isn't loaded," Earp told Taylor. "I never let my deputies carry loaded weapons when they're guardin' a prisoner. The rifle was just for show."

Taylor scowled at him. "You bastard. You're all bastards."

Earp gestured with the long barrel of the Buntline. "Drop the rifle, Taylor. Now."

The prisoner flipped the rifle, grabbing the barrel to use the weapon like a club. "Don't come near me."

Earp thumbed back the hammer of the Buntline. "It's over, Taylor. Either way, you're dead. I can kill you now or you can pay the hangman for a good knot."

Doc Bascomb peered over Earp's shoulder. "Give it up, son. The marshal is right. You don't have a chance."

Taylor hesitated but then reluctantly dropped the rifle.

Earp moved into the cell to pick it up.

Raider came behind him and stood in the arch of the cell doorway. "Hey, Earp, if that shot didn't come from the rifle, who did it come from—what the—"

Suddenly the big man from Arkansas felt iron in the middle of his back. His hand dropped for his gun but another hand beat him to the draw. Doc Bascomb cocked the Diamondback and Raider had two guns in his back.

"Tell Earp to let him go," Bascomb said.

Raider looked at the marshal, who hadn't figured it out yet. "Get him, Earp. Quick!"

Earp wrestled for a moment with Taylor. The marshal came out on top. He had the outlaw pinned to the wall with the Buntline resting just below his ear. A standoff.

"What the devil is goin' on?" the marshal asked.

Raider wondered if he was fast enough to turn on the doctor and disarm him without getting shot. "Seems ol' Bascomb here has had a change of direction. What happened, Doc? You get tired of bein' a law-abidin' citizen?"

Bascomb's voice seemed different, harsher. "You fool. You never would have figured it out if Taylor hadn't been caught."

The rush went through Raider like a flash flood. "You! You're the one. I shoulda knowed the way you were dealin' out that opium medicine."

Earp frowned, holding the prisoner in check. "What are you talkin' about?"

Taylor squirmed, trying to break loose. "Don't tell him! Keep your mouth shut!"

Earp prodded him with the Buntline. "Hold still, Taylor."

Raider turned slightly, looking back over his shoulder at Doc Bascomb. "Doc here shot the deputy in the back. What's that you're holdin', Bascomb? A pocket revolver?"

"Let Taylor go," Bascomb demanded. "Now!"

Earp's brow fretted. "I still don't understand."

"It was Bascomb that hired Taylor t' kill all those men," Raider replied. "And I'm bettin' it has somethin' t' do with Andersonville prison."

"You're smarter than I thought," Bascomb replied. "You got close to the truth, but not close enough."

"What was it?" Raider asked. "What did those boys do t' you that made you wanna torture an' kill 'em?"

Bascomb let out a hateful chortle. "Do to me? What did they do to me? There's nothing you can name, no kind of torture that they didn't do to me. Ransom was their leader. That's why I saved him for last."

"And you faked the death o' Taylor here t' throw us off the

track," Raider rejoined. "Only you didn't count on me seein' Holliday near dead from that opium stuff."

A sigh from the doctor. "That was unfortunate. But enough. Let Taylor loose or I'll kill you, Pinkerton."

"You had a chance t' kill me b'fore," Raider challenged. "How come you didn't do it when you had the chance? How come you saved me after I was beat half t' death by Ransom's men?"

"There was no need to kill you then," Bascomb replied. "You hadn't done anything to me. I'm not a killer by nature. I just wanted to even the score for what happened at Andersonville. It took me fifteen years but I was finally able to do it."

Raider tried to turn sideways. Doc Bascomb urged him around with both weapons. It wouldn't be easy to turn on the old man, not without him getting off a shot.

Earp still looked puzzled as he held Taylor at bay. "You mean the doc here was responsible for the deaths of those men?"

Raider nodded. "Yeah. He followed 'em all the way out here t' get even. Didn't you, Bascomb?"

"A long journey," the doctor replied. "But it was well worth it. I tortured them the way they tortured me. They begged for mercy the same way I did. You'll never know the pains I went through to find them. Then, when they all turned up in Tombstone. Well, I thanked God for my good fortune."

"And what about the blue army coat?" Raider asked. "Why'd you make Taylor wear it?"

"To remind them that the Union won the war," Taylor replied. "So they'd know what rebel shit they were."

Earp shook his head. "I can't release Taylor, Bascomb. And you should drop those guns and give yourself up. You're under arrest by the authority of the territorial government of Arizona."

Bascomb laughed. "Are you serious, Wyatt? If you don't let Taylor go right now, I'm going to trade his life for the Pinkerton's."

"And then I'll kill you," Earp replied. "And what do you have? Nothing. Nobody wins then."

"Let him go!" Bascomb cried.

"I can't do it," the marshal said. "I just can't do it."

"Then I kill the Pinkerton!"

Earp locked eyes with Raider. "What do you have to say, Raider?"

"Don't let him go," the big man replied. "Keep that gun on his head. If Bascomb shoots me, then you shoot him."

Bascomb pressed the iron harder into Raider's back. "You won't be so brave with two holes in you."

"Take your chances with a judge," Raider urged. "If you explain what those men done t' you, he might take it easy on you. Just send you t' prison 'stead o' hangin'."

"An old man like me wouldn't last a week in a territorial prison," Bascomb said. "No, I'm taking Taylor out of here. Nobody'll question me if I tie his hands. I'll hold a rifle on him and—"

"My men won't let you get ten feet," Earp rejoined. "They know I'd never let Taylor out of here unless I was guardin' him."

Bascomb thought about it and then replied, "All right, the Pinkerton can go with us. I'll give him an unloaded gun and—"

"No dice," Raider said. "Earp, blow Taylor's brains out."

The marshal grimaced. "What?"

Raider nodded at the outlaw. "Get this over with. Blow his brains out. Scatter his head all over this cell."

"No!" Taylor cried.

"Shut up, you coward," Bascomb cried. "Can't you see they're bluffing? They won't kill you."

"Shoot him!" Raider repeated. "Do it now. If Bascomb has the guts t' kill me, let him do it!"

Taylor whimpered like a child. "I don't want to die. Don't let them kill me. Please, don't let them."

"Shut up! Shut up!" Bascomb cried. "Let him go, Earp, or the Pinkerton gets both barrels."

Raider shook his head. "Don't do it, Earp. If he pulls the trigger, you take Taylor's head clean off."

"No," the outlaw whined. "Don't shoot me. Please."

Bascomb started to say something but there was a noise in the outer room of the marshal's office. The front door slammed. Footsteps. Raider looked over his shoulder, waiting for Bascomb to turn his head.

Doc Holliday called from the outer office. "Hey, any of you heroes home? Huh? I heard y'all—"

He stuck his face into the cell room. "What the—"

Raider saw Bascomb turn. The big man wheeled around as well, grabbing for the doctor's wrists. Taylor moved with the rest of them, trying to get away from Earp.

Bascomb had more strength than Raider figured. As they wrestled, the big man heard his gun go off. Taylor screamed and the doctor suddenly went limp, giving up the struggle with Raider.

Taylor staggered forward, clutching his chest. The bullet from the Diamondback had struck him on the left side, right in the heart. Raider snatched both weapons from the doctor and turned them on Taylor. Earp had the drop as well.

"It burns," Taylor said. "It—"

Blood poured out of his mouth. He tried to take another step but the life was quickly leaving his body. He fell face down onto the floor of the cell room. A thick red pool began to form beneath him.

Doc Bascomb knelt over the body, touching Taylor's blond hair. "No. No! You didn't have to kill him!"

Raider frowned at the old man. "What's it t' you, Bascomb? Wasn't he just your hired man?"

The old physician's eyes were hateful when he looked up at the big Pinkerton. "He wasn't my hired man, you bastard! He was my son! Taylor Bascomb. He came with me to even the score with the men who had tortured his father. And now you killed him!"

Raider figured it was the wrong time to remind Bascomb that he had been indirectly responsible for the bullet that killed his son.

Earp moved out of the cell, looking down at the body of his slain deputy. "He was a good man. We better get him to the undertaker."

The marshal went to call his other men to help with the bodies.

Doc Holliday shook his head. "Looks like I picked the wrong time to pay a visit."

Raider cast a sidelong glance at the gambler. "You couldn't

prove it by me an' Earp. If you didn't come in when you did, I might be as dead as both those poor souls."

Holliday began to cough.

Raider clapped him on the back, saying that he could use a drink when everything was finished. Holliday agreed that he needed a belt himself. Somehow, it seemed like the only way to end such a miserable day.

CHAPTER TWENTY-TWO

Raider watched the gallows as Dr. Granville Bascomb slipped the hangman a twenty-dollar gold piece. The executioner took the double eagle and promptly fixed the noose on the side of Bascomb's head, assuring the doctor that he would die instantly instead of strangling slowly, which would happen if the noose was put behind his head. The judge had sentenced the old man to hang, never taking into consideration the circumstances surrounding the murders.

When the noose was in place, a preacher approached Bascomb. The crowd murmured when the doctor refused to talk to the man of God. All of the rubbernecking spectators now believed that Bascomb was doomed to hellfire. A man who was about to meet his Maker should never shun the word of God.

Raider had to wonder what he would have done in Bascomb's place. It made him sort of sad to see the old man get it. How many men had exacted revenge on their lives, only to go free from punishment?

Marshal Wyatt Earp, who was presiding over the hanging, stepped up to Bascomb to ask him if wanted to say any last words. Bascomb nodded. Earp told him to go ahead and say his piece.

Bascomb cleared his throat and spoke in a firm voice. "Vengeance is mine, thus sayeth the Lord. I am not God, but I chose to take vengeance on those who harmed me. I have no regrets—"

The crowd tittered again, speculating on the afterlife rewards for the good doctor. Raider thought they were a bunch of holier-than-thou chicken shits. How could they know what the Creator had in mind for Bascomb?

"I lost my son," the doctor went on. "But he went on to his reward and now I go on to mine. I have prayed in the privacy of my jail cell. But now the time has come for me to die. I thank the citizens of Tombstone and the judge who heard my case. If I had to do it over, I'm not sure I'd do the same thing. But I did it and now I have to pay."

"That's right, you bastard," someone called from the crowd. "Pay up or shut up!"

A nervous laughter rolled through the spectators. Raider suddenly hated all the men and woman who had gathered for the hanging. Funny, how he took Doc Bascomb's side, even though Bascomb was a killer. The big man could not forget that Bascomb had taken him to the cathouse after the beating he had gotten at Ransom's mining camp.

Marshal Earp held out his hands over the crowd. "Let the man have his say. Next one who pipes up gets locked in my jail."

Raider found himself liking the marshal, a feeling that wouldn't last very long. He was just glad that Earp had taken up for Bascomb at the last minute. Even a condemned man had the right to say his final words.

"I know some may question what I did," the doctor went on. "But I only hurt those who hurt me. I lived as I believed. If I hurt any that did not deserve it, then I am sorry. But I say this to every man and woman in this congregation. If you believe something to be right, then you have to act on it. Even if it leads you to this sorry fate that I must now endure. If vengeance belongs to the Lord, then justice must belong to men. I only ask forgiveness of my sins, whatever they may be."

He nodded to Earp, indicating that he had finished.

The marshal offered him a black hood to wear over his head. Bascomb declined it. Earp stepped away and nodded to the hangman.

Raider saw Bascomb's body as it tensed before the drop. The big man thought the sound of the trapdoor was the worst noise he had ever heard. Bascomb swung in a circle, kicking as the life left his body. The crowd looked on, gaping at the spectacle. At least Bascomb had gone out like a man. That was all anybody could ask from death, Raider thought. The rest of it just didn't seem to matter.

Wyatt Earp pushed the bottle of whiskey across the desk.

Raider took it and poured himself another shot. It burned going down. But it was the only whiskey Earp had in his desk.

The marshal sighed, shaking his head. "Can't say I feel good about hangin' Bascomb," he told Raider.

Raider nodded. "I know how you feel."

"Usually when I rid my town of an outlaw, I can at least feel like I'm doin' my duty. But I have to say that this hangin' has left me with a funny feelin' in my gut."

"Yeah," Raider offered, "it didn't seem right somehow. At least it was over quick. The judge came into town at the right time. Two days from trial t' execution. Somethin' tells me Bascomb wanted it that way."

Earp was about to say something when the office door swung open.

They turned to look at Doc Holliday, who sauntered in and took the chair next to Raider. "Gentlemen. Big doings are over, huh? All the good citizens went home?"

Earp nodded. "It's over."

Raider offered Holliday the bottle. "Have a drink."

"Don't mind if I do."

They were quiet for a while.

Holliday finally spoke up. "Are you going to bury the father next to the son on Boot Hill?"

"Bascomb asked for that," Earp replied. "So I reckon we can oblige his last wish."

Holliday whistled through his teeth. "Yeah, that was something. Who thought ol' Bascomb had it in him to kill those men?"

"Taylor did most of the killin' hisself," Raider reminded

the gambler. "Bascomb didn't have the strength for that kinda thing. That's why I didn't suspect him, even when he was handin' out that loco juice. Bascomb confessed t' sneakin' back t' kill Ransom, though. Gave him too much o' that stuff on purpose. Damn."

"He was far from innocent," Earp said. "Far from it."

Holliday lifted his glass. "To the new town doctor. Whoever that might be. We're going to need one soon enough."

Earp cast the gambler a stern look. "Guess you'll have to live without your medicine for a while, Doc."

The gambler drained his glass. "Oh, I don't know. Raider, what say you and me head over to the saloon and find a new kind of medicine."

"Mebbe later," the big man replied.

Holliday glared at the tall Pinkerton. "Don't tell me you've lost your taste for women, whiskey, and poker?"

Raider replied that he had things to do. Write his report, send a wire to the home office, get his gear together, find a new horse. When Earp mentioned the fee for the agency, Raider told him to contact Wagner in Chicago. Any payments could be sent directly to the man in charge.

"I'm glad I didn't give up on you," Earp said. "I reckon I have new respect for Pinkertons."

"Save your respect," Raider said, rising from the chair. "We just get the job done, plain and simple."

Earp bristled indignantly.

Holliday had a vague smile drawn across his lips.

Raider left them, heading back for the stable. It was a hot day without a cloud in the sky. The kind of day when a man could feel good about himself, had he not witnessed a hanging that left a rock in his gut. Raider was tired of Tombstone, of lawmen, and of death. And even though he was glad the business had been finished, he knew it would be a while before he felt right in the deepest part of his soul.

CHAPTER TWENTY-THREE

William Wagner had been having a particularly good day before he saw the messenger boy enter the office. The lad came straight toward his desk, which meant that it was big—if not bad—news. Wagner frowned, removing his spectacles for a nervous cleaning.

"Two wires came in," the messenger boy said. "I was gonna bring the first one straight away but then the second one came right behind it."

Wagner glared at the young man. "Must I remind you, boy, that you should refer to me by—"

"*Mister* Wagner. Sorry, sir. It's just that—well, one of the messages is from Raider. And the other is from Wyatt Earp himself. He's the marhsal—"

"I'm well aware of who he is," Wagner replied, slipping his glasses into place on his nose. "May I have them, please?"

The messenger dropped both telegrams into Wagner's hand. He didn't wait for a tip. Wagner seemed more grouchy than usual.

"Boy?"

The lad turned back to Wagner. "Yes, sir?"

"See the clerk there, make sure he gives you a penny."

"Yes, sir!"

Wagner forgot about the lad, turning to the messages that had come in. He opened Raider's dispatch first, thinking that the bad news would probably come from Marshal Earp. Raider rarely got along with lawmen. He had little respect for the local constabulary.

Wagner was lowering his eyes to read when Allan Pinkerton burst out of his office. "William!"

Wagner held up the dispatches. "From Arizona. Raider has finally deigned to notify us of his whereabouts. There's also a wire from the marshal in Tombstone."

Pinkerton forgot whatever had been on his mind. "Well? Read them aloud. No sense staving off bad news."

Wagner cleared his throat. "Here goes. 'Them who was killing in Tombstone have been stopped. Earp can tell you more if you want but that is all I have to say. Send me another case as soon as you can. Raider.' Hmm. It seems as though he's wrapped things up in a neat package."

Pinkerton grunted. "Don't be too sure. Read the one from the marshal."

Wagner perused the longer message from Wyatt Earp.

"Well?" Pinkerton demanded impatiently.

Wagner shrugged. "Nothing really. He's notifying us that we can pick up our fee at the Western Union office any time we want to inform him how much he owes us."

"Why didn't Raider tell him our price?"

A slight smile spread over Wagner's lined countenance. "Well, I don't think Raider pays attention to such details."

"It's high time he did," Pinkerton railed. "What else does it say there?"

"Just that Earp was pleased with Raider's help. Says he couldn't have solved the case without him."

"Good."

"Should we request more details for our files?" Wagner asked.

Pinkerton waved him off. "Leave well enough alone. Just get Raider out of Tombstone. Put him on another case before he causes any trouble."

"I'll see to it," Wagner replied. "I'll take care of it right away."

Best to keep the big man from Arkansas on the move. Get him involved in another caper. Make sure his gun hand was kept busy. Wagner felt that it wasn't right to leave Raider idle. He seemed to get into more trouble when he wasn't working.

Wagner began to sift through his papers, wondering which case would be right for Raider's rough-and-tumble methods.

EPILOGUE

Raider rolled over on the straw mattress, opening his eyes to the fresh light of day. His head pounded from too much tequila the night before. He had been staying at the cantina for almost a week, waiting for the next assignment from Wagner. The man in Chicago was taking his good time in assigning Raider his next case. Raider was anxious to get the hell out of Tombstone. He had been staying at the cantina to avoid Earp and the other good citizens of the dusty town.

One of the Mexican women stuck her head into the room. "Señor, are you hungry?"

Raider's stomach was turning. "No. But I could use some water an' a dip in the horse trough."

"There is a tub out back, señor. If you want to take a bath, I can fill it with water."

Raider was going to tell her not to bother, but then he tried to sit up. His head ached like hell. He had been trying to drink away the memory of Doc Bascomb and his son Taylor. Raider had to wonder why the son was so much meaner than his father. Maybe the killing had just gotten to him in the end. His bad side took over, the mean dog inside him won the fight.

"What difference does it make?" he asked himself.

The woman gaped at him. "What did you say?"

"I'll take the tub, Rosita. Get to it."

"Sí, señor."

She started to go.

"Hey!"

"Señor?"

"What time is it?"

Her pretty face contorted into a frown.

"Time? The hour? Oh!" She smiled. "It's the middle of the day, señor."

"Can you be a little more on target, honey?"

"Just the middle of the day."

She ran off to fix his bath.

Raider lowered his feet to the floor. He hadn't felt so bad since his last serious head wound. Where the hell had that been? The days drifted into weeks and years and it all got muddled. When he wasn't concentrating on a case, he was usually trying to forget something horrible that had recently happened to him. Some life. Well, it was better than farming or punching cows.

"Señor?"

Pepe, the proprietor, peeped into the room. When he saw Raider was awake, he entered smiling. He liked the big Pinkerton who spent lots of money and bounced the rowdy cowboys who got out of hand. The women liked him too but for different reasons.

"Good morning, señor. I was wondering if you wanted to eat now that you have awakened?"

Raider shook his head. "But listen up, Pepe. I need somethin' else. An' I'll pay for it."

"Mi casa, su casa, señor."

"Yeah, as long as I pay. Listen, you got any whiskey?"

"Sí, I have the finest tequila—"

Raider groaned. "Not that kickapoo mescal juice. I mean whiskey. Good, strong, smooth Irish whiskey. Or Kentucky bourbon."

Pepe grinned, nodding. "Sí! And since you are my best customer, Señor Raider, there is no charge to you!"

Pepe went to find the whiskey.

Raider had to stay off the mescal for a while. It made him

feel good at first, but then about the second or third day of a bender, it always caught up with him. Maybe Pepe's whiskey would be the hair of the dog.

The Mexican woman returned and led him to the tub behind the cantina. The water was warm from the sun. Raider eased down into the tub, feeling his muscles relax a little. Pepe brought him the whiskey, which warmed his insides as well. Raider figured he might make it another day.

He soaked for a while before he noticed that everyone else seemed to be staring toward the horizon. "What is it?" he asked.

"A rider," Pepe replied.

Raider lifted himself a little, peering toward the cloud of dust that rose in the distance. "Looks like Holliday," he said. "But you better bring me my rifle anyway."

Sure enough, Doc Holliday rode up to see Raider sitting in the tub with his new Winchester in hand. The gambler dismounted in a hurry. Raider thought Holliday looked like he was in trouble.

"You all right, Doc?" Raider asked as he handed the rifle to Pepe.

Holliday coughed for a while before he caught his breath. "Raider, you got to help me. I got good news for you but I won't tell you unless you get me out of this mess I'm in."

Raider squinted at the gambler. "Is Earp after you?"

Holliday glanced back in the direction from which he had come. A second billow of dust drifted across the plain. He turned to Raider.

"She's after me, big man. And I can't seem to get away. She can ride like a cowboy and track like a Comanche. I'll never get away from her."

Raider gestured to Pepe, splashing in the tub as he moved. "You need t' go t' town, don't you, Pepe?"

"Sí, señor. I go into Tombstone every week at this time."

Raider looked at the gambler. "Doc, give your mount t' Pepe. Go on, he can ride off t' the north an' then double back t' Tombstone after a few miles. She'll chase him all the way back t' town."

Holliday grinned widely. "You're a real smart son of a buck, Raider. You think it will work?"

The big man shrugged. "I reckon we'll find out. Pepe, give my rifle t' Holliday an' ride off."

"Sí, señor. I think I know who she is and I don't want to be here anyway."

Pepe departed, stirring dust as he went.

Raider looked to the horizon again. "Better git inside. She's close."

Holliday slipped off into the house to hide.

Raider smiled up at her when she reined a black gelding by the tub. She was a fairly attractive woman with sandy hair and clear brown eyes. Deep voice. Skinnier than Raider liked them.

"You can't hide the fact that Doc Holliday was here," she accused. "Don't try to take up for him. My name is Kate Elder and I aim to find him before this day is out."

Raider shook his head. "You done caught me, Miz Elder. He rode in here not ten minutes ago an' then rode out that way."

She smirked at him. "How do I know you ain't lyin?"

Raider stood up, treating her to a glimpse of all his naked glory. "Do I look like a man who would lie, Miz Elder?"

"Men! You're all alike. Peckers with ears!"

She rode off, disappearing in the distance.

Holliday came out of the cantina, smiling appreciatively. "Good one, Raider. I owe you a drink."

The big man glared at the gambler. "You owe me some good news."

"Oh yeah. A wire came for you. You're supposed to report to a man in El Paso, Texas. Man name of Compton. Henry Compton."

"Then I ain't got time for no drink."

"Aw, Raider. You ain't gonna leave now, are you? Why—"

Holliday continued talking as Raider made ready to leave, but the gambler could not change the big man's mind. Raider knew it was time to go back to work. A man couldn't lie around forever in a Mexican whorehouse. He needed to put himself to some useful purpose. And the first step toward getting back to work was to leave Arizona and get the hell away from Tombstone territory.